Tips When Remodeling Your Home

by
William Resch

WITHDRAWN

Information to Encourage Achievement

1261 West Glenlake
Chicago, IL 60660
www.encouragementpress.com

ISBN: 1-933766-00-X
EAN: 978-1-933766-00-3

This product is not intended to provide legal or financial advice or substitute for the advice of an attorney or advisor.

10 9 8 7 6 5 4 3 2 1
♻ printed on recycled paper

©2007 Encouragement Press, LLC
1261 West Glenlake
Chicago, IL 60660

Special discounts on bulk quantities of Encouragement Press books and products are available to corporations, professional associations and other organizations. For details, contact our Special Sales Department at 1.253.303.0033.

Tips When Remodeling Your Home

About the Author

William Resch is Senior Project Manager and Chief Designer at Highland Park Millwork–an 80-year old, high-end architectural millwork company located in Highland Park, Illinois. He has been in the general contracting and millwork industries for more than 20 years, specializing in upper-tier residential renovation and millwork. Married with two children, he lives in Chicago.

Acknowledgements

Special thanks…and cheers to the following:

Luciano Ward and my family, Theresa, Madeleine, Michael & Mary

Table of Contents

Introduction

There is no greater sense of accomplishment than creating a home that is modern and efficient–one that lives up to your personal standards and the needs of your life style and family. Remodeling is one of the best legal highs there is! (In fact, some people never stop remodeling and redecorating.)

As satisfying and rewarding as remodeling is, it can also be time-consuming, expensive, nerve-racking and messy. Homeowners have a difficult time starting their remodeling projects, keeping them on budget (without creeping elegance taking over) and working with contractors, tradespeople and even lenders. No matter how big or how small the remodeling project is, there are many factors to consider, issues to be faced, decisions to be made and checks to write!

50 plus one Tips When Remodeling Your Home was written with *you* in mind. You are a homeowner and you want the best you can afford, for family and friends to enjoy, and to live in comfort. You are a couple with two jobs and personal and professional commitments that seem to consume your days. You are a spouse taking care of a family and have seemingly endless demands on your time and energy. You are single, have just bought your first condo and want to make it a home that matches your lifestyle and interests.

Whoever you are, *50 plus one Tips When Remodeling Your Home* is the book for you. You have access to practical, helpful and sensible advice from a home improvement expert with 25 years experience. You will get advice on how to:

- Get your finances in shape in order to afford your home improvement.
- Budget and plan your remodeling project.
- Find a reliable, licensed contractor at the price you can afford.
- Reduce the stress of remodeling, including keeping the kids, pets, spouse, the contractor and the neighbors all happy and motivated.
- Ensure that you are getting quality work for the money spent.
- Know whether you can do some or all of the work yourself.
- Negotiate and write a fair contract for your home improvement project.
- Know what is or is not a good investment for your home in your area.

Two major themes dominate this book which you should try to keep in mind at all times:

1. Pay strict attention to your budget and do not let the remodeling project get out of hand. It is so easy to get carried away, buying more than you should and improving the home beyond what the resale market for your home will bear. Use your tools and information in this book to control costs and to finance your remodeling project wisely.

2. Keep your emotions in check: in particular, learn the meaning of patience. Frustration can build up, often to the point of anger and lawsuits. Being upset is not going to get the job done. If you take a professional point of view, everyone else involved in the project will follow your lead.

Finally, forms and checklists are illustrated in the book. All of these forms are free to our readers by going to *www.encouragementpress.com* and clicking on the forms tab.

Happy remodeling!

Bill Resch

plus one

Remodeling:
Should You Do It?

The Challenge

Let us say that you and your house just are not getting along any more. You spend more and more time looking at the major rooms of the house, thinking about the color scheme, wondering what needs to be done to the yard, front and back. You find yourself comparing your house with others and increasingly sense that the old homestead is just not what you want.

Basically, you have three choices if you are committed to improving your home and lifestyle:

1. Tear your home down and start all over.
2. Move to a new home.
3. Remodel or rehab part or the entire home.

If you own a home with a good foundation or room to expand, the tear-down option could be an ideal solution. There can be complications, however:

- You have to move out and find temporary housing, at great expense and inconvenience.
- It will take at least 1 year to build a new home, assuming everything goes smoothly.
- The costs can be enormous—certainly $300 to $350 per square foot for new construction.
- You lose the charm of the original home.
- You may very well lose a friend or two, as people often resent the mess, inconvenience and the size of new houses.
- And then there is the stress and hassle of being your own general contractor or hiring a full-service construction company.
- Finally, there are so many decisions to make; it can almost become a full-time job.

You could move to a new home in a new subdivision or find an older home and renovate it *before* moving in. This involves many of the same issues as a tear-down; plus the fact that you now have two mortgages, or some kind of bridge financing.

Some of the issues involved in this option are:

- You may give up a cherished neighborhood or school.
- Buying one house while selling another can be tricky. Is the new house more expensive? Can you afford this?
- If you move to a newer area and you have to sell after a year or two, you may have little or no increased equity.
- How prepared is the family to move?

Your third choice is to renovate (completely or partially) your current home. There are lots of issues here–in fact a whole book full! In many cases, however, renovating can be just the ticket; you make your home more livable, more comfortable and perhaps more valuable.

Here are some of the issues renovating your current home may present:

- How much do you need or want to do and when? Do you bite the bullet and get it all done at the same time?
- What are the physical limitations of the renovation? You own only so much land on which to build and the zoning laws might not allow a third story, restrict how much land coverage you can have, or enforce strict feet to area ratio (FAR).
- Do you really need all that you want done? It is possible to do too much and make the house too expensive for the neighborhood.
- Do you and your spouse agree on the priorities and the budget?
- Do you have to move out during the construction or can you live reasonably and safely while work is in progress?
- Can you manage more stress in your life?

If renovation is for you, keep reading; we have lots of valuable advice and tips to share.

The Facts

Take a piece of paper and rate yourself (ask your partner to do the same) on the following. Use a five-point scale–one is negative and five is positive.

Your tolerance for financial risk:

1. Real estate prices will continue to rise and a home is still the best investment.
2. You are optimistic about your job security and financial stability.
3. Your credit card and other debts are reasonable at your income.

4. Financing a home improvement project is within your means.
5. As a family, you agree how much you can spend on rehabbing.
6. You can qualify for the financing you need, plus a little extra.
7. You know that costs will be higher than anticipated.

Your tolerance for time and resources needed to see the project through:

1. One member of the family has the time to manage this project.
2. You are not pressured to complete the work by an artificial deadline.
3. You understand that the work will take longer than expected.
4. You have your team assembled: banker, lawyer, architect and designer.
5. Family, friends and neighbors are available to assist in a pinch.
6. Children and pets can be managed throughout the project.
7. You will not get into arguments with the contractor.
8. You are prepared to make hard decisions.

Your tolerance for inconvenience:

1. You can tolerate major disruptions for some months.
2. There are no health reasons preventing renovation of your home.
3. You can sacrifice privacy for the sake of a remodeled home.
4. You may have to contribute sweat equity to keep within the budget.
5. You have an alternative plan should you have to move from the home during construction.
6. You understand that things can and will go wrong.

Before beginning, it is important that you understand who does what and when:

An *architect* is often the first consulted, especially on larger, complicated work. Do not attempt to design work without his or her services; besides, many city permit offices will not allow work without an architect's drawings.

A *designer* is usually hired for smaller jobs when the plan is to work within the existing space. They are often specialists. It is essential to find such help early in the process or plan on exceeding your budget.

The *general contractor* manages all aspects of the work-in-progress, including the order of work, quality control, hiring and supervising subcontractors, and obtaining building permits.

Specialty contractors are tradespeople who only do counter installation, flooring, shower stall installation, etc.

Inspectors work for the city or village and regularly visit the site to ensure that the work is in accordance with plan and code. They have the authority to shut down a project if the work is not satisfactory or if the proper permits were not obtained.

The Solutions

Plan, plan and plan some more. Advice includes but is not limited to:

Take your time. Consult with the experts and interview friends and neighbors who have performed remodeling. Look through books and magazines, stroll home improvement stores and speak to the staff.

Assemble your team. Before any documents are prepared, contracts signed or work begun, have the banker, lawyer, financial planner, architect, designer, contractor and bartender (as needed) ready to go. Make all related costs part of the budget.

Get your financing set. Be financially prepared *before* signing a contract. It takes several weeks and lots of documents and paperwork to refinance or take out an equity line of credit. Shop around and look carefully for financing. There may be hidden costs; the lowest rate may not be the best deal.

Consider doing some of the work yourself. You can do general labor, such as keeping the work site clean, tearing down and removing non-supporting walls, priming or painting walls or siding, purchasing supplies, and more.

Conversely, know what you cannot do. Do not roof the addition, rough in the plumbing or do finish carpentry if you do not have the skills. If your job is very time-consuming or your commute is long, do not fool yourself into thinking you can be the general contractor on the job site.

Prepare a list of must-haves. Focus on structural, HVAC, electrical and plumbing needs first. Windows come before marble, functionality before the Jacuzzi. Then work on the list of features you would like to have, budget and time permitting.

Set a general budget. Start with the money and work your way backwards. This is what you can afford now–what will it buy?

Get excited and get involved. See your home remodeling not as a chore, but as a great experience, despite the hardships. Get everyone in the family to be part of the team.

The Resources

Visit *www.realtytimes.com* for a variety of views on the general principles discussed. Columnist M. Anthony Carr's article, *Teardown Housing Becoming Larger Option for Homeowners,* is particularly informative and practical.

1

Controlling Your Project: Copper Gutters and Creeping Elegance

The Challenge

You have made the big decision. You are ready to go. You have decided remodeling is your best option (as opposed to selling and moving to a different house). Among the many issues you must address is how to keep the project under control, financially and emotionally. Once you start, it is easy to get completely immersed, and you may find yourself asking—What difference does it make if the project takes a month longer or if costs increase by an additional $5,000? Think carefully before you answer that question. If your remodeling costs exceed your original budget it may be the result of *creeping elegance.*

If Webster's defined creeping elegance, it would be something like this:

> *Installing copper gutters when vinyl or aluminum would do nicely; buying a Sub-Zero refrigerator even though a two-door with lots of features would suffice; laying marble instead of ceramic tiling at the front entrance…and on and on.*

Friends tell the story of the copper gutters. They rationalize the choice because these gutters never need painting; they last 35 years and cost *only* $500 more. Of course, they were planning on moving shortly, so they were not going to paint them anyway. The point is: it seemed like a good idea at the time.

Creeping elegance moves from gradual to rapidly accelerating additions. It occurs when one room is completed and it stands in sharp contrast to other rooms in the house. This is especially true when the home has an open floor plan—a remodeled kitchen next to the original family room, for example.

The Facts

The budget has to be realistic in the first place. A gourmet kitchen, installed by a professional contractor, is not going to cost $15,000 for a complete gut/rehab job. A survey of various sources (real estate data, contractor associations and regional home builders) shows typical averages nationwide:

Kitchen (225 sq. ft.) $40,000 to $45,000

What you get: a kitchen that is approximately 15' x 15', wood cabinets, laminate counter, stainless steel sink, medium-grade appliances (dishwasher, refrigerator, stove, garbage disposal and microwave), new lighting, medium grade flooring, center island, walls trimmed and painted. All of this costs about $200 per square foot.

What you do not get: marble, granite or Corian counter tops, hardwood floors, stainless-steel appliances, multiple ovens or dishwashers, and so on. A high-end kitchen may cost $300 to $500 per square foot.

Bathroom (assuming older home) $8,800 to $10,500

What you get: ceramic floor and surround, standard tub, toilet and double sinks (from the big box store), medicine cabinet and painted/wallpapered walls. A 170 square foot bathroom is approximately 7' x 10' at an estimated cost of $150 per square foot.

What you do not get: spa or oversized tub with multiple shower heads, marble or granite counters, tiled walls, new windows, sky lights, separate shower and just about everything you see in the home magazines. A high-end bathroom remodel may cost $300 to $400 per square foot.

Deck addition (200 sq. ft.) $6,500 to $8,000

What you get: an area approximately 20' x 10', pressure-treated posts and supports, composite deck flooring (simple pattern), composite rails and a small built-in (flowers or seating).

What you do not get: removal and disposal of old deck, multiple levels, curvilinear design, arbors or any other upgrades.

Family room addition (400 sq. ft.) $50,000 to $60,000

What you get: a basic room, with foundation and crawl space, tied into existing heating and air conditioning, dry wall, painted trim, prefinished wood flooring, six to eight windows, two sky lights, vinyl siding and fiberglass shingles.

What you do not get: just about everything else, including a fireplace, wet bar, built-ins of any kind, hardwood floors and trim, and a bathroom. A high-end family room could cost more than $300 per square foot.

What these estimates show you is that remodeling is expensive; none of the estimates assume anything out of the ordinary, for example:

- asbestos removal;
- new plumbing or HVAC systems;
- rewiring or new electrical service;
- foundation or structural problems;
- removing interior walls;
- damage to existing rooms of the house;
- dry rot or insect damage;
- damaged sub-flooring; or
- tuck pointing.

The Solutions

Designate one spouse as the bad cop who maintains control of the budget and checkbook. It is essential that partners agree on what the project is to entail. Before starting a project, create a simple spreadsheet with costs and estimated (amounts and dates) payouts to the contractor. Include estimated and actual amounts to spot major differences in the budget. (For more details, see Chapter 4: *The All-Important Budget*).

Add a contingency amount to your budget. This is for all the things that might (and will) go wrong. Then double that amount, just in case–especially if you are remodeling an older home. (One spouse routinely doubles her husband's estimates of a project and after the bids come in; she is usually right.) Regional differences are also extremely important factors to take into consideration when building a budget. Costs in major East- and West-coast cities will be twice as expensive as the Midwest, and the Midwest typically is more expensive than the South.

Prepare a long-term plan. Remodel the kitchen and bath year one; redo the family room year two; add a room year four, and so on. By doing so, you will ensure that you have the financing (either saved or arranged) when needed. If you know that the family room is next, you will be less tempted to instruct the contractor to continue the work at a time when you are neither financially nor psychologically prepared.

If you have not, hire an architect. You can get professional design and specification help at home supply stores, specialty stores or by working directly with your contractor. If the contractor is experienced, he will have seen it all. Listen to his advice, even if it means spending a few dollars more (emphasis is on *a few*) in certain areas–for example, flooring, countertops and cabinets.

Avoid financing your remodeling project with a charge card. If you use a credit card for purchasing materials, make sure you pay it off in 30 to 60 days. A good rule of thumb to follow is: If the job costs less than $10,000 to $15,000, pay for it from savings or from current income. Larger amounts are best financed through a loan or home equity line of credit.

Remember to factor in all costs. Permits, architectural drawings, dumpster rental, rubbish removal and other unanticipated expenses can add up quickly. It is important not to underestimate these costs.

Before remodeling, look carefully at your current financial status. Do not take on a project if your current credit card and mortgage debt is equal to or greater than 50 percent of your income. Pay off your existing debt first, reduce your projected expenses or put off the remodeling for a year while you save for the project.

The Resources

Pre-arranged financing: You do not want to run out of money and stop in mid mess nor do you want the contractor to place a contractor's lien on your home for non-payment.

Detailed wish list: Spend the time to know exactly what you want, down to the smallest detail. Buy magazines and design books and walk the aisles of home improvement stores.

Talk to friends and neighbors who have been through remodeling: Learn from their mistakes, ask them what they did right (or wrong) and what they would do differently.

Bids: Get at least three estimates from qualified, licensed contractors and a budget based on these estimates.

Patience and good humor: A must!

2

Getting Your
Finances in Shape

The Challenge

Home renovations cost money. The problem is, you do not have an infinite supply, and what you do have needs to be used for everyday expenses such as food and utilities. This book advocates a responsible (conservative, if you will) view on money matters, including budgeting and financing. There is absolutely no point in taking on additional debt (which you may not be able to afford) just to have a new kitchen. Nor should you think that the future value of your home justifies major expenses in the near term. Your home may grow very quickly in value, but unless you are going to sell, you cannot solve the short-term need for liquidity.

Consider the practices of lenders and credit card companies, including car dealerships, which begin their sales pitches by trying to determine what you will accept as monthly payments, not what you can afford. Essentially, the current environment is nothing more than a vast credit trap; little emphasis is placed on the creation of wealth through investments, savings and home equity.

Advertisements on television frequently offer mortgage or financing options, including 100 percent equity loans, usually at a higher rate and on the assumption that property values will continue to grow. Other options offer an interest-only loan, with little or no equity built up during the period of ownership. Again, it is based on the assumption that housing values will continue to rise.

If your renovation project is built on this kind of financing, it is on shaky ground. The goal here is to discuss prudent alternatives and to prepare to finance your renovation so that you can repay the money on a timely basis.

The Facts

Household debt in the United States is nearly $10.3 trillion, an 11 percent increase over last year. That is an astonishing amount of money, but as long as the economy grows and home prices increase, consumers should have no difficulty managing the situation (according to former Federal Reserve Chairman Greenspan). However, everyday consumers are having a great deal of trouble managing this amount of debt. Not all home prices grow at California rates each year. And in many cases, income (especially if you have lost a job) cannot keep up with debt load.

Lenders expect consumers to have short-term debt (for example, credit cards, department store accounts and short-term loans) that is less than 20 percent of gross income. So if household income is $60,000, then you should be under $12,000 (still a good deal of debt to manage).

Long-term debt–mortgages and lines of credit secured by your home–should not be more than 28 percent of your gross income (in fact, financial planners and lenders will accept from 25 percent to as high as 30 percent). For your household with the $60,000 income, that means the mortgage payments cannot exceed $18,000 a year, first and second mortgages combined.

Many consumers are unwilling to sit down and do some simple analysis and planning: do you know what you owe and, just as importantly, do you know how much it costs to live each month? Are you aware of what your credit report says about you? Under the Fair and Accurate Credit Transactions Act (FACT Act), you can receive a free credit report once every 12 months from each of the three nationwide consumer credit reporting companies: Equifax, Experian and TransUnion (see The Resources at the end of chapter).

Do you know what your credit score is? The higher your credit score, the better your chances of financing your renovation with a loan carrying a good interest rate. Some of the variables that determine your credit score are:

- Length of time on the job; the longer the better.
- Monthly income; the higher the better.
- Debt percentage of take-home income (30 percent or less).
- A paid-off loan from this lender.
- Current bills not past due.
- Length of time at current and former addresses.
- A checking and savings account.

In short, the lender is looking for stability and a proven history of your ability to repay your home improvement loan.

The Solutions

You need to decide how important your renovation project is. Is it more important than a great vacation, a new car, dining and entertainment, or other of life's pleasures? If so, and you cannot finance the entire project through savings (which would be ideal), then you must prepare to borrow by getting your financial life in order.

Begin with high-interest credit cards. There is no secret that credit card debt strangles many consumers, even to the point of their borrowing from one card to pay other credit cards, sometimes called *suicide rollovers*. The more credit cards you have, the more you can borrow to pay back other debt–an endless cycle that leads to bankruptcy court.

Some simple steps to regain financial control:
- Stop buying with credit cards.
- Use a debit card or cash. When you run out of cash, you cannot buy any more.
- Pay off the card with the lowest balance first; then cut it up.
- Once a card is paid off, it frees cash for paying off the other cards.
- Limit the number of cards you own. Two for personal use and one for business would seem reasonable.
- Do not apply for store credit cards.
- Do not pay for meals with credit cards.
- Pay off what you spend on a credit card each month.
- Never pay just the minimum.
- Debt consolidation usually does not work and often gets you further in debt.
- Use savings in low-interest bank accounts or money market accounts to pay off debt. What you earn on the money is usually far less than what you are charged by credit companies.
- Refinance your home if the costs of refinancing are not higher than the savings.
- Do not spend a bonus or tax refund. Save it for your renovation project or pay off credit cards.
- Always pay yourself first, then your bills. Automatic withdrawal into savings or investments is ideal. You never touch the money and are never tempted to spend it.
- If you get a raise, bank the new money each month.
- Buy what you can afford and afford what you buy. If you want the new room addition, you may have to forgo the $50,000 SUV. You decide the priorities.

One method of getting your financial house in order is to sell assets to pay down debt. You may have assets of which you are not aware. Take a look at the silver tea service from your aunt twice removed on your mother's side. What about insurance policies? The investment portion of a whole life policy pays next to nothing. Talk to your agent and see if this is a sound idea.

How many sets of golf clubs, power tools, kitchen appliances and bicycles do you need? Sell them on eBay. Remember: eBay sales have to be legal and as advertised.

Everyone hates the B word, but even a limited-time budget is an excellent tool. There are a number of good books that address this subject. See The Resources below for Websites with free fillable budget forms.

The Resources

To obtain your credit report, you can click on *www.annualcreditreport.com*, a centralized service for consumers to request annual credit reports. It was created by the three credit reporting agencies to facilitate customer requests.

You also can contact the three major credit reporting agencies directly:

- Equifax at 1.800.685.1111 or *www.equifax.com.*
- Experian at 1.888.397.3742 or *www.experian.com.*
- TransUnion at 1.800.888.4213 or *www.transunion.com.*

If you would like to understand how expensive it is to pay just the minimum on your credit cards, go to *www.bankrate.com* and click on the tab marked Credit Cards for a variety of calculators that will show you how disastrous making minimum payments can be. There is a lot more at this site that can help you achieve sound financial management.

Also visit *www.consumercredit.com* sponsored by American Consumer Credit Counseling (ACCC). The site has objective recommendations on books, workshops and web seminars. You can also sign up for their free dollar-stretcher newsletter which helps you live better for less.

The Center for Debt Management at *www.center4debtmanagement.com* is a huge resource, much of it free of charge, designed to help people reduce debt, develop a budget and expand their financial knowledge.

3

Getting the
Financing You Need

The Challenge

You have started on your budget, wish list and a host of other details. Now you need to determine what you can afford, not just on a cash flow basis, but also in terms of your long-term goals. Let us assume that you are also saving for retirement, perhaps college educations or other major needs. Do you spend it all now and/or use up your borrowing base, or do you keep some in reserve for future needs?

The best source of financing is your bank or credit union, where you can withdraw money from a savings or money market account and pay for the work as completed. The recommendation of this book is that if your project costs between $10,000 and $15,000, you should pay in cash, not through further borrowing.

If you need to or decide to borrow additional funds, how does that fit into your current mortgage situation? Are you prepared to refinance your mortgage? Would a home equity line of credit be a better choice? Did you just refinance to take advantage of changing interest rates and would further refinancing be very expensive? Are you hurt by current interest rates? That is, if you have just refinanced, and rates are rising, will your mortgage plans be affected by actually increasing the cost without any real benefit to you (like more money at good rates)?

It is possible that your net borrowing could reduce your equity below the 20 percent standard set by lenders, at which point you would be required to pay for private mortgage insurance (PMI), which is expensive and not tax deductible.

The Facts

Because your goal is to have financing arranged before a single nail is hammered, you need to think about how lenders view your situation.

Lenders use a simple debt-to-income (DTI) ratio to determine if you can take on more debt for your renovation project. For example, if you have a gross monthly income of $5,000 and your current mortgage payment is $1,250 (this includes real estate taxes, insurance and PMI, if any), your DTI is .25 ($1,250/$5,000 = .25). This DTI is called the *front-end* ratio as it includes only housing costs. In theory, your lender would allow for some modest additional borrowing, assuming that your front-end ratio does not exceed 28 percent.

Another measure used by lenders is the *back-end* ratio: housing costs plus all debt found on your credit report. (Once again, this demonstrates the need to get credit card and other installment debt in manageable shape). Assume the same gross income of $5,000 and $1,250 for housing costs, but then include $900 of credit card/installment payments. Your total DTI is 43 percent ($1,250+900/$5,000 = .43). A DTI ratio of 43 percent would disqualify you for further borrowing as the banking standard is often around 36 percent of income. Possible solutions to this problem:

- Postpone the renovation project.
- Pay for the changes in cash.
- Increase income.
- Reduce debt.

The DTI is not an absolute on the part of lenders. Various loan programs have different criteria, and may or may not subscribe to a strict interpretation of DTI ratios. Credit card debt could be consolidated into a larger loan; other income could also be considered.

Lenders can also be preoccupied with your credit score which qualifies you as a low-or high-risk borrower. Your credit score is a guideline used by lenders to measure your credit worthiness—a prediction of sorts of how you will repay your debts. It is common for a lender to charge a high-risk (meaning a poor credit rating) candidate a higher rate than someone who has a higher credit score.

The three major credit reporting agencies use the same criteria to generate a credit worthiness score. Scores range from a low of 500 (assigned an F grade) to a perfect 990 (assigned an A grade). Few borrowers are at either end of the spectrum. Your lender will give you some idea of what credit score is expected to gain the best rates.

The Solutions

There are many different types of loans and mortgages available from banks, savings and loans, credit unions and mortgage companies. An often forgotten borrowing source is private individuals, even family and friends. Many well-heeled investors will, for a secured interest in your home (a second or third mortgage) lend money at a favorable rate. The same is true with family members who are looking for investments that pay more than anemic money markets or savings plans.

Here are a few loan options:

Fixed rate mortgages: You finance (or rather refinance) your entire real estate debt through a loan of definite term. The advantage is that you know your payment will be the same (except when taxes and insurance go up) and that the interest rate will never change through the life of the loan. Further, these loans can usually be prepaid to reduce the term and interest charges over the life of the loan. Extra payments to principal can have a dramatic effect on total interest paid. The big disadvantage is that if interest rates go down, you are paying more for the loan than you need to.

Adjustable-rate mortgage (ARM): As the name implies, the interest rate can change (usually annually) and rates are typically based on short-term Treasury securities. Interest rates in the beginning are usually lower than a fixed rate mortgage and are best used if you think interest rates will come down. There is both an annual cap and a life-of-a-loan cap on ARMs. If interest rates go down, you can convert to a fixed rate mortgage.

Balloon mortgages: This is a variation of an ARM, with payments based on a fixed mortgage for a period of time, at which point a single large payment (the balloon) is due. Again, rates are lower in the beginning, and when the balloon is due, you can either pay it off or refinance. This kind of loan is a gamble: when the balloon comes due, you may have much higher interest rates or your financial condition may have worsened.

Sub-prime loans: These loans are for people who cannot qualify for traditional loans at favorable rates, either because of high DTI ratios or poor credit histories, or both. The name tells it all: much higher rates because you are a risky candidate.

Interest-only loans: These allow you to pay just the interest on the loan, nothing toward principal. Lower payments allow for higher amounts to be borrowed. Ironically, the more you borrow, the more beneficial these loans are. So, if you borrow $500,000, your savings by not having to pay the principal would be substantial. Interest-only loans would not be very useful for a $100,000 loan, as the amount saved would be insignificant. At some point, your interest-only period will be over and you have not reduced the principal by a penny. You must then refinance, pay the entire balance or start paying off the balance with a higher monthly payment.

Graduated payment mortgages: Not only do you not pay principal (like interest-only) but you pay only a portion of the interest. This is negative financing (amortization), in that your unpaid interest does not disappear, but becomes part of the loan. So if you borrow $300,000 this way, in 5 years it is possible to have a loan balance of $352,500. If you decide to sell after the 5 years and your property has appreciated 10 percent to 15 percent per year, this kind of financing might well be worth it.

This discussion is just the tip of the iceberg. The quality of the lender, the service provided, your relationship with a personal banker and the fees charged for loans and related services are all part of the equation. Shop carefully for a lender with the right program for you and do not fill out multiple loan applications; it can hurt rather than help your renovation efforts by damaging your credit score.

The Resources

If you have an existing relationship with a banker, he or she is the best source for renovation financing. They know you, at least on paper, and have half the paper work needed on file already.

Online sites like *www.lendingtree.com, www.QuickenLoans.com* and *www.eloan.com* offer a variety of services—of course, the majority are related to home and renovation loans. You can learn a great deal about how the whole system works if you take the time to visit *www.freddiemac.com.*

The U. S. Department of Housing and Urban Development (HUD) has a variety of loan options and services, especially if you own a fixer-upper. HUD's 203(k) loan program is especially suited for this purpose. To learn more, visit *www.hud.gov.*

The All-Important Budget

The Challenge

Throughout this book, the subject of a budget is repeatedly emphasized because renovation is so expensive. From one point of view, there are two legitimate ways to go about the process:

1. Bid the specifications for the job, then get financing.
2. Work out the budget and build to budget (the recommended approach).

While the budget is the key to a successful renovation, it cannot be prepared until you take a realistic assessment of your financial position. This includes making conservative estimates of your future earning power, the value of your property and your current and future obligations–including saving for retirement, emergencies and education for your children.

At this point, assume that you have your financial house in order, that you qualify for the financing you need and that you can afford to make the payments now and in the future. (Other chapters provide a primer on credit repair, getting out of debt, the types of financing available, and more.)

Because the budget must include some contingencies, the total amount of available funds is not an absolute number for renovation. If you qualify for a $75,000 home improvement loan, that does not mean you automatically have $75,000 for construction. There are loan and home appraisal fees. There may be design or architectural costs, and legal and permit costs. And you must set up a reserve fund for unanticipated problems. Deduct those immediately from your budget and set them aside.

In this example, we have set aside:

$3,000 for financing fees.
$6,000 for the architect.
$1,500 for legal and permit charges.
$7,500 (10 percent minimum) for unknown problems.

Your actual construction budget is now a more modest $57,000. What will this amount buy you?

The Facts

Your overall goal is to pay out the fewest dollars for the most work to be paid over the longest period of time, while borrowing the smallest amount of money at the lowest interest rate. Yikes! Assume your $75,000 is a line of credit on which you can write checks as needed. Similarly, you are then billed for partial payment next month and the following months at the going interest rate. Every month (every day in fact) that you do not have to take out money from your line of credit, you reduce the cost of borrowing and reduce the cost of the renovation.

Because borrowed money for home improvements is usually tax deductible (check with your tax preparer to make sure), many consumers feel that they are not really paying interest because they get some relief through the tax system. To a point this is true, but the less you are in debt, the less it costs. Do not focus on next year's tax return; focus on real costs for real money at real interest rates.

It is not a good idea to write a check for the full $75,000 from your line of credit and put the money in your checking account (or the even the money market account). Interest charges are always greater than what you would earn from the bank in checking, savings or money market accounts. Borrow as you need it and not a day before.

Even though you have stipulated a $75,000 budget, you have already exceeded it by the very fact that you are borrowing the money. The budget increases by definition by the interest rate charged and the length of the term of the loan. The real cost of the project is $102,183 (monthly payment of about $851), assuming a 10-year payoff at an interest rate of 6.5 percent. If your interest rate is higher and your term length longer, you will pay even more.

Every dollar not borrowed, every dollar paid from savings, every dollar borrowed at the latest date possible reduces the real cost of the project. The project should not be based on what the lender says you can afford, or the so-called monthly payment, but the real costs in dollars over the life of your loan and your ownership of the property.

The Solutions

Your budget, then, determines not only what you expect to pay for materials and labor, but when you expect to pay it out. Use a simple spreadsheet like the one shown on the next page:

Home Renovation Budget				Date:			
Item	Amount budgeted	Amount paid	Date due	Date paid	Total paid to date	Difference
Architectural fees working drawings changes final drawings permits bonds						
Borrowing costs loan origination closing costs appraisals						
Building permits changes inspection demolition variances						
Contingencies						
Labor appliances cabinets/built-ins decking dry wall electrical finish carpentry flooring HVAC insulation landscaping lighting masonry painting plumbing roofing rough carpentry siding windows						
Legal fees						
Materials appliances cabinets/built-ins decking dry wall electrical finish carpentry fixtures flooring HVAC insulation landscaping lighting masonry painting plumbing roofing rough carpentry siding windows						
Upgrades						
Totals:						

The spread sheet can be used in a variety of ways. First and foremost, it serves as a record by which you can estimate the costs as you go about doing your initial planning. As you narrow down choices and make decisions about what will or will not be included in your renovation, you can record the expected expense based on second-phase research and comparison.

Once you have agreed on specifications and have a final bid from the contractor, you can then use this document as a financial planner, recording what will have to be paid when, how much and any variance experienced. If you are really strict about your budget, variances will have to be covered somewhere. Perhaps you have enough in your contingency category to cover the unexpected increase in costs of flooring or cabinets. Alternatively, you may reduce the quality of the counter tops or lighting in order to make the budget balance.

The Resources

Several sites have interesting approaches to money management. Visit *www.moneypants.com*. While a fee-for-service site, it offers a money management tool not just for renovation, but for your entire financial life. Similarly, you may find *www.foxway.com* useful, with a variety of free budgeting forms and useful calculators. It also has a good deal of paid advertising and clearly intends to sell you a variety of services, from loans to insurance. Also *www.saygoodcredit.com* and *www.letsrenovate.com* have electronic tools which can be adapted for home renovation budgeting.

Use the construction cost guide that the contractors use, the *Bluebook Residential* and *Light Commercial Cost Guide*, to understand the real costs of construction. Visit *www.bluebook.net*

The budget spreadsheet illustrated on the previous page is available as a .pdf download free of charge if you visit *www.encouragementpress.com*

5

Outpricing the Neighborhood

The Challenge

How often have your friends and relatives said that the house they just bought or renovated would be the last house they would ever own? Or this time, they are going to do it right and will never again move? This is *the* house!

More often than not, that you-will-never-move-again attitude changes. Ultimately, that lovely, newly renovated house is going to be sold, either because of a life-style change or for economic/employment reasons. Will it happen next month, next year or in 10 years? You do not know. But you have to consider what the planned renovations will mean when you sell.

There is evidence that homeowners are overbuilding when renovating houses. The average size of a home has nearly doubled in the last 20 years. If everyone in the same neighborhood is doing the same, and values remain high, there is no problem. In some neighborhoods and suburbs, this is what is happening–there is little risk and even less exposure to the vagaries of the real estate market.

But it is not always so. Many homeowners are, in fact, becoming speculators. Their willingness to expand and to improve a home is based on the current belief that housing prices will continue to rise. Of course, no one wants to predict a fall in housing prices, and no one can predict such a change with any certainty. However, the current environment suggests real estate prices in many markets are slowing, though the bubble predicted by certain experts may not be a reality.

For some homeowners, price stabilization is nearly as disastrous as a bubble if they are forced to sell soon after renovating a home in which they had invested large sums for enhancements. The improvements made were based on longer-term economic assumptions; if, however, you lose your job or have to move for any reason, there is a chance that you have overbuilt because the price of housing has not caught up with your remodeling costs.

Changing or improving neighborhoods pose similar risks if the real estate market slows and the rate of appreciation does not support your level of renovation and improvements. Who is going to buy the house with a 1,500 sq. ft. addition when the neighborhood has stopped changing and appreciating?

Having said all this, not everything need be considered in cold dollars and cents. Renovation involves other reasons than money: stability, schools, church, a growing family. But even these intangibles must be tempered with some sense of economic reality.

The Facts

The latest figures from the Federal Government suggest that last year the average home price appreciation was 12.2 percent more than the year before. That is an astounding figure if you own a home—and a scary percentage if you wish to buy a home. As a rule, it supports the current theory that putting money into real estate, specifically renovating your home, is well worth it.

However, be aware that there are big regional differences:

Pacific Coast	17.33 %
South Atlantic	16.90 %
Mountain	16.23 %
Middle Atlantic	12.42 %
New England	9.43 %
East South Central	7.06 %
West North Central	6.55 %
West South Central	6.07 %
East North Central	5.99 %

Even within regions, considerable discrepancies exist: Chicago is undergoing a building boom and has much higher appreciation than the rest of the East North Central region. The same is true for Boston (New England) and other regional, metropolitan centers.

There is strong evidence that this report reflects the peak in real estate appreciation for a while. In other words, do not renovate solely on the basis of this impressive data.

Be realistic not only about the total dollar amount you plan to spend in relation to what the neighborhood will bear, but also about the specifics that you will spend your dollars on. As previously mentioned, if your improvements are too personal, you will not recover their cost. Other costs for improvements that may never be recovered might include:

- Swimming pool;
- sauna or steam room;
- greenhouses;
- gazebos;
- elaborate landscaping;
- outdoor kitchen;
- built-in aquariums;
- elaborate home theatres;
- wine cellars; and
- any improvement that reflects personal taste vs. necessities.

Consumers assume that bath and kitchen improvements always pay for themselves at the time of resale. One study suggests that is not always true (see The Resources at end of chapter).

The Solutions

The best way not to over-improve is to get to know your neighborhood or suburban housing market intimately. Local real estate agents who have been in the business for 10 years or more are the best source of information about prices and trends. Ask two or three to give you a market analysis of your home prior to renovation; as part of this, you will get *comps* (similar houses that have sold in your price range). An experienced agent will not try to inflate the value of the home because should you engage her at some future time, her words might come back to bite.

Visit every open house you can. Evaluate and compare your house to others that you have visited. It is difficult to be objective–and easy to rationalize that your home is bigger, better and fancier than your neighbor's, which is selling for $50,000 more than you would have thought, leading you to believe that your home must be worth more. Planned improvements budgeted for $100,000 can easily be justified in your own mind, but not so easily in the open market. It is essential that you make the important distinction between what a house is appraised for and what it actually sells for.

As a rule, do not be the first in your area to add substantially to your home. Let others take the risk and test the renovation waters. Home improvements and major renovations tend to go in waves. While you do not want to go passively with the flow, multiple and major renovations within a few blocks or within your subdivision are a pretty clear indicator that the real estate prices have upside potential and that similar additions or renovations will match the market.

There are two exceptions to this rule: If you bought the cheapest house in the area and if you bought the most expensive. In the former case, your upside potential and thus your ability to recoup renovation is substantially higher than the average. In the latter, the reverse is true: you already may be at the top of the market and further improvements are unjustified from a resale point of view.

Watch for changes in retail stores and outlets in our area. If major companies are moving in and stores and restaurants are more upscale than in the past, it usually indicates that the marketplace has acknowledged that your area is up-and-coming. In some large cities, gentrification is obvious when developers come to an area, tear down under-used retail or commercial property and build combined retail and residential property.

The county assessor's web site, if there is one, is a great place to compare and contrast, helping you to determine what the market will bear. Often, you can see at a glance what the housing stock is like and get a description of what the house contains (3 baths, 5 bedrooms, fireplace, driveway, 10 rooms all together). If a number of the houses are larger than in the past, the renovation move is on.

The Resources

The Office of Federal Housing Enterprise Oversight (OFHEO) has a house price calculator that will assist you in getting a *general* idea of the current value of your home. Be careful, though, as regional and local differences can be huge. Visit *www.ofheo.gov/Landing.asp* for more information. Two additional sites that offer values of homes in your area are *www.Zillow.com* and *www.RealEstateABC.com*.

A good, general site for those interested in renovating, buying or selling a home is *www.realestate.com*. In the learning center, you will find a short article about which renovations pay or do not pay for themselves.

Remodeling
Fraud

The Challenge

Consumers are victims of fraud so frequently that it is almost impossible to track the numbers in any meaningful way. The three biggies are banking, identity and home improvement/remodeling fraud. By current estimates, these and other forms of fraud costs consumers several billions of dollars a year. This figure only covers those amounts that are actually reported to the police and consumer watchdogs; many consumers never report fraud because they are embarrassed to admit that they got swindled.

Some forms of fraud are subtle, allowing contractors, lenders, suppliers and others to bilk consumers over a period of time. Such fraud can be hard to spot; perhaps the sums are not that large.

Even with all the preparation as prescribed in this book, fraud is a very real possibility when you engage relative strangers to work for you with a budget of many tens of thousands of dollars. There is an obvious temptation to take advantage of the situation, especially if some level of trust has been built up. Fraudulent contractors usually are one step ahead of consumers and their advisors. New scams and deals that are too good to believe are constantly perpetrated on the elderly, the unsuspecting, the hurried and distracted, the desperate and the poor.

Fraud is not limited to just builders and contractors. Brokers, bankers, suppliers and even consultants can also be involved. In many cases, the scam is directly tied to renovations or repair through some form of home equity scamming. You could lose your home and your money if you borrow from unscrupulous lenders who offer you a high-cost loan based on the equity you have built up.

The Facts

Simply stated, fraud is an intentional deception which results in some unfair gain to a third party. It is not always just money; materials, labor or financing can also be at the root of the fraud.

There are many levels of fraud:

- False advertising.
- Over-billing for materials or services.
- Charging for materials paid for by another customer.
- Substituting inferior goods for what is specified.
- Palming off inferior goods as a brand name.
- Bait and switch–substituting a remodeling plan you can afford for one you cannot.
- Changing contract terms after the fact.
- Not giving consumers time to consider their choices.
- Threats or intimidation–e.g., you will not get this work completed before winter.
- Falsifying information–e.g., saying that the foundation is unstable when it is not.
- Forging documents.
- Misrepresenting credentials or the amount of time in business.
- Providing made-up or paid references to support a contractor's claims.
- Lending institutions charging fees for services not required.
- Referrals to lenders from whom the contractor receives a kick-back, and vice versa.
- Purchasing more materials than required.
- Failure to perform all or part of the agreed services.
- Failure to fulfill warranty obligations per the contract.
- The list goes on and on...

Are contractors more dishonest than other business professionals? Probably not; but it can be more difficult to spot the fraud. For example, do you really know how many 2 x 4s or sheets of plywood are required for your work? Did you pay attention to whether the contractor used one inch sheeting rather than three-quarter inch material? Do you know for sure that the cabinets specified are the same grade as were installed? Are all the materials new or did some of them come from a demolition from an upscale home?

As a general rule of thumb, you can assume that the longer a contractor has been in business, the less likely the possibility of major fraud. Most major scams come from those who enter and leave the industry quickly, as they have no future in the business.

In addition, consider some of the strategies that lenders tied to renovation projects used to defraud homeowners:

Equity stripping–you receive a loan based on the equity in your home, not your ability to repay based on your income. You lose your home for nonpayment.

Loan flipping–you are encouraged repeatedly to refinance your loan, often including more money that the original loan. Each time you refinance, even if you receive a lower rate, you pay additional fees and points.

Credit insurance packing–your loan includes credit insurance, which you may not need.

Bait and switch–you are offered one set of loan terms when you apply for your renovation loan then find that the documents contain a higher rate than anticipated.

Deceptive loan servicing–you are not given accurate information about how much you owe and how much you have paid already, allowing for the possibility of overpaying your loan.

The Solutions

The best solution to preventing fraud is to take your time. Do not be pressured by sales people, contractors, your spouse or yourself. Read and review the documents, check the references thoroughly, see work in progress, check banking references, call the insurance agent to find out what coverage the contractor has purchased and for how long the policy has been in place.

Ask for references for work from 2 or 3 years ago, rather than last week or last month. Stability within the industry is the key. Specifically ask for references from homeowners who have used this contractor for more than one job. The highest praise is reserved for those contractors whose customers are satisfied repeatedly.

Conduct your own occasional audit, especially if your project is lengthy and therefore very expensive. There is always going to be some overage and underage when ordering materials for a job. Bricks break, tiles crack, wood is warped or miscut; two sheets of extra dry wall is not fraud. Fifty sheets more than you need stored in the company truck should raise an eyebrow. If you have questions, ask about the situation immediately.

Focus on the expensive materials like doors, windows, cabinets, appliances, slate or marble. Anything copper is worth looking at twice: pipe, flashing, gutters and downspouts. These items are expensive commodities. The same is true of high-end millwork for interior trim around doors, windows and chair rails.

One of the oldest tricks, especially if you are satisfied with the work and the experience, is for contractors to ask for additional money at the end of the job. They will insist that material prices went up, that labor costs were more than anticipated, that the job was more complicated than first bid, etc. Some or all of these facts may be true. But unless you have agreed to exceptions in writing, resist the pressure. This relationship, no matter how pleasant or friendly, is a business relationship, based on a contract.

Do a basic credit check on your contractor *before* you sign the agreement. He or she will probably do the same on you. Ask for and expect banking and supplier references. It is easy enough to see if there are any funds in a business account: call bookkeeping and tell them you have a check for $5,000 and ask if it will clear the bank at this time. (Of course, they will not tell you the balance in the account.)

Home improvement financing fraud is best avoided by going through a reputable lender–a bank or financial institution that you currently use. If you negotiate the deal carefully, watch junk fees and ensure that the documents you sign reflect the terms and conditions of your financing, you should have no problems. When you interview the lender, get a written commitment to terms–especially expenses and fees associated with the loan. Make sure you understand who pays for what–home appraisal fees, title fees, loan origination fees, etc. Know the type of loan you are getting–fixed, variable, no-documents, interest-only–and ensure that what you asked for is what you are getting.

Seek professional help; ask your lawyer or accountant to review the documents, terms and conditions. You have the right to cancel if you smell a rat.

The Resources

The Federal Trade Commission has two worthwhile self-tests for consumers. Visit *www.ftc.gov/bcp/conline/edcams/homeimp/quiz1.htm* and *www.ftc.gov/bcp/conline/edcams/homeimp/quiz2.htm*.

To file a complaint, visit *www.homerepair.about.com* for a link to the FTC homepage. There is even a sample letter you can use to file your complaint. Visit *www.fraudaid.com* for a variety of resources, including a dictionary of financial fraud terms.

7

The Architect Is
Your Best Friend

The Challenge

Architects come in all different shapes and sizes. You need an individual who specializes in residential construction or rehabilitation.

Practicing architects generally have a Master's degree in architecture and are certified through the National Council Architectural Registration Boards (NCARB). As part of this certification, architects take a qualifying exam and are required to keep their certification up to date through continuing education courses. Architects are licensed on the state level, so some may be required to have special training.

Even when you narrow down a pool of architects who specialize in home construction or renovation, it is essential to find an individual who fits your style and taste and is licensed to practice in your community. Further, you want to find an individual who will work well with you, and not try to impose his or her style and ideas on you.

The Facts

What do architects do for you and why are they so important?

The first part of the question depends on the complexity of the job. At the very least, they can provide the rough drawings (later refined by the architect, a designer or the contractor). The rough drawings are essential if you need a permit. And at this stage, keep them rough—why spend money on a complete set of drawings if there is a possibility that you will not get a permit for the proposal or that variances are needed?

The architect will prepare the finished or final drawings. These let your contractor know exactly what is to be done, what materials are to be used and the level of quality you require. Of course, the final drawings are essential in bidding out the job with your pool of qualified contractors. In addition, the drawings and details prepared by an architect will become part of the contract, the ultimate protection for homeowners.

You may decide to hire an architect to ensure that the contractor is completing the work according to code and to the specifications prepared by the architect, and fulfilling the expectations you have as to the finished project. Typically, an architect would charge a percentage of the total construction budget to oversee a project to completion; 5 percent to 7 percent is the norm. On a $125,000 construction budget, that can add $6,200 to $8,400 to the cost of renovation. Is this amount reflected in your budget?

Find an architect who speaks plainly, and who can help you understand terminology and the reasons why features are or are not included in the final plan. You should be able to read the blueprints as well as the contractor. Expect assistance from your architect. Ask questions about why some features were not included, the choice of materials and more.

Most architects charge by the hour for both design and drawings for your project. A very rough price range is $100 to $150 per hour. There are big regional differences, and if you choose a nationally known and renowned architect, expect much higher rates. The clock starts when the architect sits down with you to discuss your ideas and plans and, of course, any subsequent changes you make are billed at the going rate. This is yet another reason to know your own mind.

Changes when construction has begun can be a double whammy—new drawings and specifications, as well as removing what has been built and starting over. You may also have to go back to seek approval from the city and revise your permit. The architect (or designer) is your best assurance that you have your concept firm in your own mind. They should be able to run down a series of questions, once they have interviewed you and presented drawings. Make changes, if you must, but make them as early in the process as possible. New computer software will allow the architect to show you what the room or addition will look like, even allowing you *to walk* the room and see it from various angles.

The Solutions

Finding an architect to assist with your project offers some of the same challenges as finding a contractor. Some are better on design while others excel on the technical side of the project. Where do you need help most?

If you do not plan to make major changes to your home, designers can be a financially attractive alternative. They often specialize in a particular functional area—e.g., bathrooms, kitchens or basements. Perhaps you will use both: find a good technician as an architect and leave the design work to other specialists. Many home improvement stores have design help available as part of the purchase or for an additional fee.

The American Institute of Architects (AIA) is a good starting point for finding your architect. You want someone who is local, someone you can afford and is compatible with your project.

When searching for your architect, the best sources are friends, relatives, neighbors, real estate agents and colleagues. Even with a referral, you may find that after the interview, an architect is just not right for you. However, he or she may recommend a colleague, or even a competitor, to take on your job.

Finally, check with your town's building department. They know the local architects and have usually inspected their buildings and are familiar with their work.

The interview is absolutely fundamental. You want to ask about qualifications, experience, background, rates, types of services and more:

- Do they handle new construction, renovation or restoration or all three?
- What experience do they have for large, complicated jobs?
- Can they recommend a contractor with whom they have worked?
- What kind of design technology do they have at their disposal? CAD-CAM Design programs can save a lot of time and money.

Ensure that the architect's license is current and that the references provided are checked carefully. Most architects have an extensive portfolio of projects on which they have worked and will happily lead you through them to demonstrate their skill and background. If possible, visit the actual sites where the architect has worked. Interview a contractor who has worked with the architect.

Checking references includes a review of state and local licensing boards. They will have a record of disputes or consumer complaints.

Architects often take on too many projects at one time. Ask about their current workload and what that might mean in terms of your renovation. Ask for a completion date for rough drawings as well as final drawings. Ask who is going to do the actual work; if the architect you are using is a firm, associates and assistants may do the actual work with your architect handling only the final review. This may not be what you want.

An architect's help will be essential if you anticipate a variance in local code or wish to modify a residence in an historic district. You cannot take on these governing bodies by yourself. (You may not get what you want even with an architect's help; nevertheless, your odds improve greatly.) If the changes desired are particularly sensitive, you may wish to find an individual who has had experience working with an historic district council.

The fundamentals of a contract apply with architects as well as with contractors. See Chapter 10: *The Contract That Binds: Most of the Time* for a discussion on contracts. Some local companies combine the services of architects and contractors into a full-service operation. Consumers find this concept very convenient and the companies often do excellent work. As a rule, expect to pay more to cover marketing and overhead expenses. These companies can easily be checked through the better business bureau in your area. They, too, will be happy to show you the portfolio of completed projects.

Like any other business transaction, communications is essential: know what you want, communicate your ideas and insist on regular reports on progress. Do not hesitate to show the architect your budget. He or she may tell you right off the bat that your plans and budget do not match.

The Resources

Consumers can find a variety of inexpensive, easy-to-learn and easy-to-use design and building software on the market. The value is that you may be able to reduce the design or architectural costs by reining in your expectations before you get to the architect and being better able to communicate what you want in the first place. Visit *www.amazon.com*.

Visit the American Institute of Architects' Website at *www.aia.org*. While the site is designed specifically for practicing architects, it is a fine source of information.

8

Finding a Contractor: Better Than Doing It Yourself

The Challenge

If there is a single, paramount concern for consumers when considering remodeling a home, it is the daunting task of finding an honest, dependable, licensed and fairly priced contractor.

The problem is compounded in a hot real estate market where the demand for qualified individuals is extremely high. If you really want to get a project going on a timely basis, you might have to take a chance on a contractor simply because everyone else is booked.

An extreme example is provided by a customer who wanted extensive and expensive millwork (windows, woodwork, flooring and doors) for his very up-scale residence. However, people and facilities were working 6 days a week, 10 hours a day to keep up with current demand. This customer ended up writing a check for $100,000 to get on the list for future delivery—in 2 years!

When demand for services is high, new people enter the contracting industry. While this may relieve the demand for services, it does not necessarily guarantee consumers a good deal. A large part of the problem with some people in the construction industry is misrepresentation—some of it intentional, some not and some even well-meaning.

Intentional misrepresentation can take many forms:

- Contractors who ask for fees up front and never return.
- Those who come to your home to sell you more than you can afford.
- Individuals who are not contractors at all, but handymen with limited experience.
- Contractors who have credentials in one area, but say they can do it all.
- People who misrepresent insurance, bonding and licenses.
- Contractors who offer bogus references.

- Tradespeople who start a job and never finish, either out of fraud or mismanagement.

Well-meaning, but still misrepresenting the facts:

- Those who misrepresent the amount of backlogged work they have already.
- Contractors who promise a finish date before the holidays.
- Individuals who are dependent on substandard subcontractors.
- Contractors who are poor managers, and lack equipment or trained personnel.
- Tradespeople who are part-time, but give the impression that they are full-time.

Many years ago, my wife and I hired a contractor (whose real career was as a bricklayer) to do general renovation on an 80-year old house; he had worked with some of our relatives, mostly to build new fireplaces and repair older ones. Our relatives found that he was generally competent for smaller general repair and replacement work, especially tiling baths and entrances to the house. Naturally, we felt that he qualified to do the same work for us. So, he was hired.

Naturally, creeping elegance (or the desire to do more that we had planned set in.) The bricklayer, now contractor, hired a small crew to do demolition, build interior walls, dry wall, install kitchen cabinets, add a bathroom and more. Our *strategy* was to work with him on a time and materials arrangement. We had no written contract, except an agreement to pay him a specific hourly rate and his assistants a different rate.

It became virtually impossible to track hours or judge productivity. Multiple afternoons were spent at the lumber yard to pick up materials. He had no formal training in planning larger projects, so each day's work required a trip to the store. Progress was slow and expensive some days; the work often did not begin until 10 a.m., or later. A qualified contractor would have completed the work in half the time. The cost may have been higher, but the work would have been consistently better and we would have had our evenings to ourselves!

Did it work? Yes and no. Frankly, we were lucky. The contractor became our guest each evening, settling down for multiple cocktails (and expensive Scotch). Hours and money due were recorded on slips of paper, and subsequently lost. Years later, long after the work was completed, the contractor was financially hard-up and asked for additional payment. We assumed that the bill had been settled long ago. This lack of records or a contract proved to be a double-edged sword, as his claim could not be verified.

The Facts

An informal survey of the business section of a big-city newspaper over a 3-month period showed that contractors and builders were among the most frequent business petitioners for bankruptcies. Home remodeling is a business that is relatively easy to enter, without proper experience, licenses or training. Let the buyer beware.

Does the size of the contractor's business mean that you have a qualified, competent company? Not necessarily. There are many local, boutique companies or partnerships that are highly qualified. A large, regionally recognized firm probably has a larger pool of resources, more current technology and better labor pools–and more to lose if you are unhappy. Also, the costs of such companies could be perhaps double those of a smaller organization. (They have higher overheads, support staff and marketing expenses that justify the higher bid.)

Not surprisingly, contractor fraud and other problems are high on the list of complaints with organizations such as the Better Business Bureau, the local Consumer Affairs Office and the State's Attorneys Office. As their chief complains, consumers report shoddy workmanship, unfinished work and the inability to make contact (by phone, fax or e-mail).

When looking for a qualified contractor, do *not*:

- Consider phone or door-to-door solicitations.
- Pick a name from the phone book.
- Respond to a casual referral.
- Hire family members (assuming you want to be on speaking terms).
- Rely on Internet sites.
- Ask the local handyman.

And do *not* use contractors who:

- Ask you to get the necessary building permits.
- Provide no workmanship warranty (for 1 year).
- Offer a bid for the job on the back of a business card.
- Have no formal place of business (home office is an acceptable alternative).
- Have only one specialty for general renovation.
- Offer a discount if you find other customers.
- Just happen to have materials left over from another job.
- Insist that you make an immediate decision, without competing bids.
- Ask for no charge for the work because your home will be a demonstration for marketing.
- Are only willing to accept cash or insist on upfront payment.

- Offer very long guarantees.
- Want you to borrow from a lender that he or she recommends.

The Solutions

Always get more than one, detailed estimate: in fact, get three for larger jobs, making sure that the contractors are bidding on the exact same specifications. Do not alter a single item; otherwise you cannot compare the estimates.

References are essential: not only get two or three, but also ask for references for work that you can actually inspect. People want to be helpful; often they will invite you in to see the work. Even if you cannot get in, you can drive by and see the outside construction. Press for details when you contact the references. Inquire about schedules, cost overruns, use of subcontracts, neatness of the job site, workers' punctuality, etc. Ask if the homeowner would recommend the contractor and if they would they use them again.

Make sure that your contractor is licensed, bonded and insured. Ask for copies of the insurance policies. Also find out if they use sub-contractors, who will be in charge of your job on a daily basis and the best time to reach them to talk about the work and problems, if any.

Take the time to learn the different trades and specialists: finish carpenters, electricians, HVAC installers, plumbers, masons, roofers, drywallers and a host of people will all be part of your life. Know what they do and in what order they come to your site.

The Resources

The best ways to find a qualified contractor:

- Satisfied friends, neighbors and relatives.
- Jobs in progress where you can inspect the work in progress.
- The National Association of the Remodeling Industry.
- National Association of Home Builders (*www.nahb.org*) for local members.
- National Kitchen and Bath Association (*www.nkba.org*).
- National Contractors (*www.NationalContractors.com*).
- Angie's List (*www.angieslist.com*).
- Contractor's License Reference Site (*www.contractors-license.org*).
- National Association of the Remodeling Industry (*www.nari.org*).
- Real Estate.com (*www.realestate.com/learning-center/default.asp*).
- Respond TM Home Services (*www.remodeling.respond.com*).

9

Communication
Is the Key

The Challenge

There are many circumstances, almost all of them bad, that start with poor communication and, even worse, unrealistic expectations on the part of the homeowner and the contractor. Consider the following examples:

- The contractor first agrees, then decides not to, take on your work.
- The project did not start on time.
- The work has stopped for no apparent reason.
- There is no communication between sales, estimating and the foreman on the job.
- A finish date was missed for no apparent reason.
- The contractor calls only at night or on the weekends.
- A change order was not executed.
- The homeowner does not know the right questions to ask.
- English is a second language for one or both parties.
- The homeowner insists that the project be managed his or her way.
- A disagreement turns into a shouting match.
- The contractor is rarely on the job site.
- There is no paper trail, written contract or other supporting documents.
- The contractor's phone, fax or e-mail is either busy or full.
- You speak to the contractor only through an assistant.

There is another side as well. The contractor is available, but:

- Decisions about changes are delayed because you cannot make up your mind.
- You do not understand the language of remodeling and construction.
- Payment has not been made as promised.
- Spouses or partners argue and disagree about the details of the renovation.
- Phone calls are not returned.
- Materials or work are rejected unreasonably.
- The homeowner is haughty, condescending or complaining.

- Expectations are greater than the budget.

And the lists goes on and on.

Some problems may never be solved no matter how frequent the communication. These kinds of complications center on expectations: you thought this and the contractor assumed that. Short of litigation, someone is going to have to give.

Contractors also report that homeowners often focus on only three issues: the start date, the finish date, and the cost. Nothing else seemingly matters. Be smarter than this. Yes, these three are important, but the devil is in the details. Take the time to learn and communicate those details, and expect the same from the contractor.

The Facts

When you start your renovation and the relationship with your contractor, bear in mind that:

- His experience and education are different from yours.
- Recognize and accept the differences.
- Small mistakes and variances from plan are an indication that there is a communication problem.
- Your contractor is not always wrong or the bad guy.
- Your contractor has legitimate issues which you must address.
- Your contractor has a right to make a profit (unless he has grossly underbid the project).
- The contractor's past methods of communicating with a client may not work for you.
- A contractor's availability is limited to reasonable business hours; your availability is also limited.
- The contractor may not be on the job site every day, every hour of every day.
- Other jobs are in progress besides yours.
- You and your spouse can and will give conflicting information at times.
- Changes in work orders after the contract is signed cost money.
- Your contractor should be as concerned about safety and an orderly job site as you are.

Because the agendas of the builder and homeowner may be different, you need to make sure that clarifications on key issues are absolute. Consider some simple, but common situations reported by the National Association of the Remodeling Industry, among others:

- Homeowners believe a finish date is a firm date, but reasonable delays for reasonable reasons must be discussed before the job begins. Bad weather, change orders and unforeseen problems are not the contractor's fault. For

these reasons, few contractors will sign a contract with a late penalty.
- Honest and open discussion of the details is a must. Will heavy equipment be stored on the driveway or lawn? What about broken or damaged personal property? Who will pay for these items and whose responsibility is it to ensure that they are not in the workspace in the first place?
- If you live in the house during construction, a good deal needs to be clarified about how the household operates during construction. Decide:
  - If radios are allowed on the job site and how loud.
  - If workers may use your phone for personal use.
  - What the working hours are, start and finish (some municipalities have rules on when construction can start).
  - If workers may use the bathroom(s) in the house–and if so, which ones?
  - If food and lunches may be taken on the job site.

These are just a few of the everyday practical issues that need immediate clarification. Once the job starts, it is going to be difficult to communicate the need for changes.

The Solutions

The emphasis throughout this book has been that every major item in your renovation process needs documentation. The overall solution is to develop a system whereby all the details are organized and on hand when needed.

Your biggest responsibility in this process is to learn what questions need to be asked throughout the remodeling, but particularly before the contract is signed and work has begun. Make a list; be thorough and specific.

Simple working files should be kept at the job site and a copy at work. That way, when calls come from the contractor, everyone is reading from the same page. The file should be organized by date. All notes, drawings, change orders, copies of checks, budgets, even printed copies of e-mails should be included. Everyone should know that this file exists. The contractor can check details, add to the file to keep it current, learn what has and has not been paid for, etc. Let this file be the contractor's as well.

When a decision is reached, a change noted, a problem discussed, make a summary of the conversation and add it to the file. Tell your contractor that you will add this summary to the file.

Schedule regular meetings to discuss the day's goals and go over any problems that need clarification. Ask for the names of the subcontractors or individual workers who will be on the job site. If the contractor is not on site daily, who is in charge? Make sure have everyone's phone, fax and e-mail address. Determine what times are available and convenient for meetings and phone calls.

You may need to have a translator or someone who has second language skills around at all times. This will help you be more comfortable communicating with workers and sub-contractors.

Overall, you want to know who will be on site and what they are doing that day/week. You will want to know what the goals are for this week, if the project is on schedule and on budget–and if they are not, why not, and how this can be remedied? Make it very clear to the contractor that your budget is fixed. A clear statement of what you want done, the completion date and the agreed price cannot be repeated often enough. The time will come when the contractor will want to discuss further payments; you will have your files and budgets to resist the pressure.

Should a major problem arise, insist on a face-to-face meeting, and ask a trusted friend, advisor or even your lawyer to attend as a witness. A third party can also act as mediator and suggest a solution.

Make sure that you have all construction and permit documents. You paid for them and should ensure that they are in order. The contractor is not going to pay any fines–you are.

Schedule a final walk-through with the contractor and his foreman to finalize a punch list of everything that needs correcting. Go through the work area ahead of time, several times if needed, using a checklist and the original plans or drawings as an aid. Take your time preparing for this meeting and the walk-through. Schedule a completion date and a final meeting to ensure that everything on the list is finished.

Make it clear that the final portion of the payment will be held until the list is completed. The warranty process should be reviewed and put in writing in case materials or workmanship become an issue once the contractor is off site. Keep the warranty process in your records and give a copy to the contractor.

The Resources

There are any number of good books available that will help with communication and project management. If you visit *www.amazon.com* or other online booksellers, you can find such helpful titles as *People Skills: How to Assert Yourself, Listen to Others and Resolve Conflicts* (Touchstone, reissued edition) and *Complete Idiot's Guide to Project Management*, 3rd Edition (Alpha, 2003). Both books are well received by customers.

10

The Contract
That Binds:
Most of the Time

The Challenge

Phase one of the hunt for a contractor is just about over. The next item on the agenda is a contract, letter of agreement or some written document that puts the deal together. Oral agreements, except for very small amounts for repairs, are not an acceptable alternative; neither are e-mails stating terms and conditions. You need to have a paper trail for money transactions, including construction work.

You cannot formalize an agreement without prior, mutual understanding of the general terms and conditions of the project. So have your wish list all set, your budget prepared, your architect working and financing arranged. Place special emphasis on the schedule early on–your job is probably just one of many projects in progress for the contractor.

Alarm bells should ring if you have difficulty arranging an initial meeting with the contractor. Use this first meeting to set the tone of the relationship: friendly but business-like. Be respectful of the contractor's need to run a business and earn a living. You are obviously anxious to get going and enjoy the improvements; on the other hand, a schedule needs to be realistic.

The Facts

Many contractors have prepared documents with boilerplate language in which details are included on a separate schedule (an addendum). If correctly done, all of these pages become part of the formal contract. For many small- and medium-sized jobs, these pre-printed forms are fine. As a rule, the more complicated (and more expensive) the project, the greater the need for detail and clarification in a formal contract.

You do not have to use the contractor's form. With the help of your lawyer or legal forms supplier (see The Resources at the end of chapter) you can submit a document that is more to your liking. A contract has common features in order for it to be enforceable:

- There must be an offer–in this case, a promise to perform remodeling work.
- An offer must be accepted, usually by both parties signing the agreement.
- There must be proper consideration; typically a stated amount of money to be paid.
- The signers of the contract need to be 18 years of age and competent.
- There is nothing fraudulent or illegal in the document.
- An agreement cannot be signed under duress or threats.
- The contract is void if a party dies.

You cannot accuse the contractor of non-performance if you prevent him from doing his or her job as scheduled. For example, if you fail to make the premises available or have not moved the furniture out the room (as agreed), the contractor cannot start the job. Essentially, you have frustrated the intent of the contract, and cannot say that the performance was substandard or late.

If there is any doubt in your mind, get your lawyer involved.

The Solutions

Your contract should include:

- The contractor's business name, address, phone and e-mail.
- Business license number, including bonding and insurance information.
- A complete description of the work and materials specified exactly as agreed.
- A schedule for payment, including the amounts to be paid.
- The total cost of the work, including any interest or other extraordinary charges.
- When the work is to be started and be completed, and any penalty for failing to comply.
- The contractor's responsibility for building permits and inspection of the work.
- Any warranties on workmanship and materials.
- Some statement that the builder is an independent contractor.
- A statement in favor of mediation and/or mandatory arbitration.
- Under what conditions the contract can be canceled.

Never leave blank spaces in a contract–they might be filled in later to your detriment. Cross out and initial any blank spaces in the form. Have the contractor initial the crossed-out blanks.

A contract may have a number of supporting documents–schedules, specification of materials, additional work orders, budgets, etc. These documents must be referred to in the contract (for example, See Schedule A for list of materials used). Attach them to the basic document, and initial and date each supporting page (ask the contractor to do the same). This ensures that additional sheets or documents are not added to the contract or replaced with others without your knowledge.

When signing a significant contract, you might consider signing the contract with a witness present or asking a witness to sign the document as well. The contractor will expect all parties to the agreement to sign–husband and wife, co-owners of the property and so forth. In addition, they typically want all concerned parties to be present at the initial meeting, as well as any important subsequent meetings. This is basic, good business in that everyone will stay on the same page throughout the renovation.

If you are seeking legal help or if you feel that you need additional time to study the document, postpone signing the contract. Do not feel pressured to sign. Make sure that you want and can afford this renovation. When the contract is signed, make multiple copies of the final document. Keep one as a working document and the signed original in a safety deposit box or with your lawyer.

A contract can be and often is modified; make sure such modifications are in writing. A contract can also be canceled. Consumer law (Federal Trade Commission's Cooling-Off Rule) allows you to cancel a contract for services within 3 business days after the sale–with a full refund of any monies paid. Contractors should provide a cancellation form; if you do not receive one, a certified letter postmarked within 3 business days will generally be sufficient. Saturdays are business days; Sundays and federal holidays are not. The contractor has 10 days to return or refund any money paid or to cancel any note for payment you may have signed.

More about warranties: a warranty is basically a promise on the part of the contractor to stand behind the completed work. It is not unreasonable for the warranty to extend from 6 months to 12 months after the work is finished. A full warranty (a promise to fix a problem within a specified amount of time) is the goal. Be cautions about limited warranties, which may cover the replacement of defective materials, but not the labor involved.

Part of your agreement should include a document called a *lien waiver*. Essentially, this prevents any subcontractor placing a mechanic's lien on your property because your general contractor did not pay them. Without this waiver, you could be responsible for paying the plumber or painter, even though you paid the contractor for the services. You cannot sell or transfer property if there is an unsatisfied mechanic's lien.

Ask your builder to provide a rough schedule of when the various trades will be on site. If you are participating in the work in any way, this will help you plan and organize your tasks. For example, if you are buying supplies and materials, you want the rough plumbing supplies to be there when the plumber shows up. On the other hand, you do not want to take on any expense before you have to, or to clutter the work site with materials that might not be needed for weeks. Ask who will be in charge of the site each day or for the entire project. The same person on site will ensure a better renovation.

How much should you pay upon signing the contract? As little as possible. Negotiate hard on this point. Do not pay the entire amount up front; do stagger payments to completion dates. Always reserve a portion of the payment until the entire job is finished.

Finally, is daily clean-up part of the contract? You will learn more about the daily routine in later chapters, but clarification on this crucial function is essential.

The Resources

Various vendors supply contracts and other basic legal documents for a nominal sum. Try to find one that is state-specific if your state has very strict construction/remodeling laws. If you buy a form online, make sure that it is fillable and savable. Some forms can be filled in electronically, but not saved. Visit *www.socrates.com* or *www.uslegal.com*.

Visit *www.bbb.org* for a variety of quality consumer information as well as a means to find your local Better Business Bureau. Also, consider *www.ftc.gov* for good, general consumer background information.

Learn and understand the basics of the law: the *Socrates Practical Law Handbook: Solutions for Everyday Legal Questions* (Socrates, 2006) is highly recommended. The most expensive alternative is a good lawyer, experienced in contract negotiations and construction agreements.

11

Forms: Sample Contractor Agreement

The Challenge

Throughout this book, one theme has been constant: the need to write a clear, concise and legally binding contract whenever you employ contractors, subcontractors, designers, architects or other suppliers of services. While many contractors will come prepared with their version of the document, you do not necessarily want to use it. It is entirely possible that the document is written in such a way as to be very advantageous to the contractor–to the detriment of your wallet.

The Facts

All contracts constitute an *offer*. Signing the document confirms your acceptance of this offer. There needs to be *proper consideration*–typically, a stated amount of money is paid for the work. The signers must be competent and of age (18 years or older). The contract is void on its face if it contains anything that is fraudulent or illegal, and it cannot be signed under duress.

The Solutions

On the following page is a sample of a standard contract used by a construction company for home renovations.

Standard Remodelers Contract

This is not a legal document. You may download this information freely. However, do not use this document without legal advice.

A REMODELING CONTRACT between _____

_____ (the Owner[s]) and _____ (the

Contractor), which parties, for good and valuable consideration, agree as follows:

1. DESCRIPTION OF WORK: The Contractor agrees to complete the addition/remodeling project on the building located at _____ described as follows in Appendix A: (a description of the project and a copy of all final plans and/or specifications).

2. PAYMENTS TO THE CONTRACTOR: The Owner(s) shall pay the Contractor the sum of $___ _____ (the contract price) for the work described in this contract. The contract price is payable as follows:

a. A deposit of $_____ is due when this contract is signed.

b. The Owner(s) shall pay the Contractor a portion of the contract price based upon the Contractor's percentage of completion as described in Appendix B. The Contractor will verify, in writing, the percentage of work completed.

c. All payments are due within five days of the date the Contractor's invoice or request for payment.

d. Upon notification by the Contractor of completion of the project, the Owner(s) shall prepare a punch list within _____ days. Upon completion of all items on the punch list, the Contractor is entitled to the balance of the contract price.

3. ALLOWANCES: The contract price includes allowances for the following items as described in Appendix C. The allowances include both materials and installation unless expressly noted otherwise. Any selection which costs less than the allowance may be used as a credit to the contract price at the end of the project. Any selection which exceeds the applicable allowance shall be treated as a change order in accordance with paragraph 6 of this contract.

4. TIME OF PERFORMANCE: The Contract shall commence work within _____ days of the date all required permits or other approvals are issued and the Contractor receives the deposit as described in paragraph 2 of this contract. The Contractor shall diligently pursue and substantially complete all work under this contract within a reasonable period of time taking into consideration weather conditions, delays in the selection or availability of materials and any change orders.

5. CHANGES TO THE CONTRACT PRICE: The contract price may change due to latent defects in the existing structure including, but not limited to, soil conditions that may require extraordinary work, the presence of asbestos materials, inadequate structural support for the addition/remodeling project or damage to the existing structure (termites/wood rot) which could not be observed by the Contractor prior to commencement of the work or location of the project within a flood zone which requires additional design and construction. If the Contractor encounters any such latent defects, the Contractor shall immediately notify the Owner(s) and shall prepare an estimate of the increase in cost. Any costs incurred in preparing the estimate (such as engineering fees) shall be paid by the Owner(s). The Owner(s) and the Contractor shall sign a written change order for the increase in the contract price. If the Owner(s) does not wish to pay the increase in the contract price, the Owner(s) shall pay the Contractor all costs incurred in connection with the project.

6. CHANGE ORDERS: If the Owner(s) request a change in the scope of the work, the Contractor shall prepare a written change order which shall reflect the increase or decrease in the contract price. The change order must be signed by the contractor and one of the Owner(s) and the Owner(s) must pay the Contractor any such increase before any work on the change order shall begin. The Owner(s) shall not direct any of the Contractor's employees,

subcontractors or suppliers to make any changes without the Contractor's express written consent.

7. LIMITATIONS INHERENT WITH ADDITIONS/REMODELING PROJECTS: The Owner(s) understand and agree that there are certain limitations inherent in any addition/remodeling project that do not exist with new construction projects. Based on that understanding, the Contractor's performance will be evaluated on the following construction standards:
a. The Contractor will use his best effort to patch any damage to the existing structure but that the patching may be detectable.
b. The Contractor will use his best effort to match any new materials with the existing materials used in the structure but the difference in the materials may be detectable.
c. The Contractor will use his best effort to minimize damage to existing driveways, landscaping, lawns and any other existing improvements on the property. The Contract price includes allowances for the repair or replacement of any such items. The Contractor's responsibility for any damages to such items is limited to the amount of the allowance.

8. DANGERS INHERENT IN ADDITION/REMODELING PROJECTS: There are certain dangers inherent in addition/remodeling projects because the Owner(s) usually occupy the structure while the work is ongoing. The Contractor will take reasonable efforts to secure the job site at the end of each work day. The Owner(s) understand the existence of these dangers and will take all reasonable precautions to avoid these dangers. The Owner(s) are solely responsible for any injuries to the Owner(s), members of the Owners' family, invitees or trespassers on the project during the term of this contract.

9. INSURANCE REQUIREMENTS/RISK OF LOSS: The Contractor shall maintain workers' compensation insurance and liability insurance for damages to persons or property who enter onto the job site at the request of the Contractor. The Owner(s) are responsible for all other insurance requirements including casualty insurance in an amount necessary to cover the improvements to the property as a result of this contract. The Owner(s) shall bear the risk of loss for all materials incorporated into the structure or stored on the job site.

10. CONTRACTOR'S WARRANTIES: The Contractor makes no warranties, expressed or implied, except as expressly stated herein:
a. The Contractor warrants that all materials will be new materials unless otherwise specified and that all materials and labor shall be warranted for a period of 1 year from the date the Contractor gives the Owner(s) notice of substantial completion.
b. The warranty on any appliance or equipment supplied by the Contractor is limited to the warranty provided by the manufacturer of such appliance or equipment.
c. THE ABOVE STATED EXPRESS WARRANTIES ARE IN LIEU OF ANY OTHER EXPRESS OR IMPLIED WARRANTIES, INCLUDING THE IMPLIED WARRANTY OF FITNESS OR HABITABILITY.

11. OWNER(S) RESPONSIBILITIES: In addition to all other duties of the Owner(s) under this contract, the Owner(s) shall have the following responsibilities:
a. The Owner(s) warrant the they have fee simple title to the property described in paragraph 1 and the Owner(s) shall provide the Contractor with adequate access to the property required by the Contractor to perform this contract.
b. The Owner(s) are responsible for obtaining all approvals required by any architectural control committee or homeowners' association.
c. The Owner(s) are responsible for obtaining all required soil tests prior to the Contractor commencing any work.
d. The Owner(s) are responsible for obtaining all boundary surveys, foundation surveys, or final surveys required by the lender.

12. FORCE MAJEURE: Contractor shall not be liable to Owner(s) for any loss, cost or damage resulting from or arising out of a delay or inability to perform this contract caused by any force majeure such as: acts of God, declaration of war, fire, flooding, strikes, accidents or other similar events.

13. DEFAULT/NOTICE OF DEFAULT: Contractor shall be in default under this contract if he shall abandon work on the structure or otherwise refuses to carry out his obligations under

this contract (unless such abandonment or refusal is based upon a prior default by Owner(s) which Owner(s) have failed to cure after notice thereof). Contractor shall be deemed to have abandoned work if he or any subcontractor shall fail to perform any work on the structure for 21 consecutive days, unless such failure is the result of any force majeure. Owner(s) shall be in default under this contract if they shall refuse to permit Contractor to complete his performance, shall fail to pay any amounts when due, or otherwise refuse to carry out the obligations of Owner(s) under this contract (unless such refusal or nonpayment is based upon a prior default by Contractor which he has failed to cure after notice thereof). In the event of default, the other party shall give the defaulting party written notice, by certified mail return receipt requested or by hand delivery, which specifies the event(s) of default. The defaulting party shall have ten (10) days from receipt of the notice in which to begin the curing of any default, which actions shall be continuously pursued and completed within a reasonable time in light of the nature of default; provided, however, the cure of any default in payment is limited to ten(10) days from the date of notice of default. If such default is cured within the time specified, each party agrees that this contract shall remain in full force and effect and neither party may assert any claims as the result of such default.

14. REMEDIES AFTER DEFAULT: In the event of default by either party which is not cured within the time specified, the non-defaulting party may seek specific performance, or declare the contract terminated and seek damagers for breach of contract from the defaulting party. In the event of default by Owner(s), Contractor shall be entitled to all costs incurred to date plus liquidated damages in the amount of $_____, without regard to the stage of completion. The parties have agreed to this liquidated damage amount due to the uncertainties associated with the damages which Contractor may incur as the result of default by Owner(s).

15. GOVERNING LAW: This contract shall be construed and enforced in accordance with the laws of the State of _____.

16. INTEGRATION CLAUSE: The contract constitutes the complete agreement between the parties and shall not be modified except in writing by all parties hereto.

17. HEADINGS: The headings on each paragraph are for convenience of the parties and shall not be construed to alter or amend any provisions of this contract.

CONTRACTOR _____   OWNER(s)_____

Print_____   Print_____

Signed _____   Signed_____

Title _____

Date _____   Date _____

Signed _____   Signed_____

The Resources

To gain access to these and other forms throughout this book, visit *www.encouragementpress.com*. There is no registration required. All forms are free to our readers. You can include your e-mail address to learn more about other Encouragement Press books and products.

Visit *www.socrates.com* for a variety of quality business forms related to your remodeling and construction needs. All forms are sold as downloads.

12

Warranties on
Work and Materials

The Challenge

After spending a great deal of money on renovating your home, there is always a bit of buyer's remorse—we could have done this, we should have added that feature, etc. But most of all, there is a genuine concern about the durability and long-term satisfaction of the work done, materials used and the appliances and fixtures installed.

The best way to ensure your peace of mind is to sign a contract with a reputable contractor. This is easier said than done, of course. But having read the chapters dealing with contractors, you should have a written warranty that in theory protects you from future problems.

As you will soon learn, a warranty is not always a warranty as most people understand it. Further, warranties can be complicated. But even if they are clear-cut, getting satisfaction based on the warranty may be difficult.

The Facts

A warranty is basically a promise on the part of the contractor or the supplier (home improvement store) to stand behind their completed work or materials and products supplied. Federal law requires that a warranty be made available before or at the time of purchase, so it would typically be presented by the contractor at the time you sign a valid contract.

In the case of materials, appliances, HVAC systems and other major components to a home renovation, you have the same rights—to see and read a plain-English version of the warranty (many manufacturers now make the warranty available in Spanish and French as well). A basic warranty should include all of the following:

- Name, address and phone number of the maker.
- What is covered under the warranty and what is not covered.
- Length of the warranty and what you need to do in case of a problem.

- If the warranty covers replacement, repair or refund, and if there are any costs to you.

Warranties can be full or limited. With a full warranty, the supplier or manufacturer will fix or replace the item at no cost, or a full refund will be provided to the buyer. Limited warranties usually offer free parts, but not labor, so there is some expense to the buyer. Warranties rarely cover what is called *consequential damages*–that is, the seller would replace a washing machine if defective, but not the damaged clothes that were in the washer. Of course, in such cases, you always have the option of going to small claims court to try to settle the matter in your favor.

In the course of renovation, a phrase you often hear is–I will take care of that later. This is, in effect, an oral warranty and has no legitimacy. If you feel that you need a specific statement dealing with a specific matter, get it in writing and add it to your general warranty.

During renovation, it is important to distinguish who is responsible for services and materials: the contractor or the original manufacturer. For example, a new, state-of-the art Sub-Zero freezer is part of your kitchen specifications. Assuming that it has not been damaged during installation, the contractor does not assume full warranty for the appliance. Rather, it is the manufacturer's responsibility.

On the other hand, the contractor is responsible for the materials and installation of products that he buys and provides for the job. For example, if the specifications for flooring call for ¾-inch substrate and ½-inch tiles on top and the contractor uses ¼-inch substrate and ¼-inch tiles, then he or she is responsible.

Any reasonable contractor will offer some kind of guarantee that if a problem occurs (or becomes apparent) only after you take possession of the house, it will be repaired at full cost to the contractor. As a rule, this additional warranty will be for 6 months. New home construction warranties may extend up to a year, though given the many variables not under the contractor's immediate control, this is probably unrealistic unless it is a major, structural element, such as the foundation.

You may choose to negotiate with your contractor for an extended warranty–for example a small payment every 6 months for the next 2 years, after which normal wear and tear would begin to set in. Normal wear and tear is a real problem. Even if a complaint is filed during the term of the written warranty, the contractor might say that the problem is not bad workmanship or defective products, but ordinary use (or abuse). Prepare yourself for these situations, because it is a matter of interpretation and persuasion as to who should replace the defective work or materials.

One of the most frequent complaints about remodeling contractors is that they do not do what they say they will do after the job is finished. In short, homeowners call and call, and problems remain unsolved. The contractors often seem reluctant to honor their commitments and warranties. The reason is simple economics: it is very expensive for the contractor to send a crew, large or small, to your home on a Saturday to repair the tile or reset the grout or touch up the paint in three rooms. If they stall, perhaps the problem will go away. Do not let it go away. Be persistent.

What motivation does your contractor have to make good on the warranty in your contract? Other than good character, he has almost none–unless you help to motivate him. As a businessperson, a contractor depends heavily on word-of-mouth advertising. This is where the advantage shifts to you. Make it clear that you will not offer to be a reference for future business and that, if necessary, you will file a formal complaint to the local Better Business Bureau and/or the city consumer affairs office.

Many manufacturers of appliances and other home systems offer extended warranties on everything from microwave ovens to new furnaces. An extended warranty offers consumers protection in that if something goes wrong after the manufacturer's warranty has expired, you will have recourse to get the item repaired or (rarely) replaced. Should you get an extended warranty? Well, they can be pricy relative to the cost of the item purchased, so as a rule, the less expensive the item is, the less valuable an extended warranty. An extended warranty makes no sense for a microwave or small appliance; it might make a great deal of sense for a high-end appliances or the new whole-house vacuum system.

The Solutions

Your first and foremost protection takes place at the contract stage. Make sure that the warranty is clear, concise and unambiguous. Never take an oral warranty, as it is unenforceable.

You do not need to send all the separate warranty cards to every manufacturer if the offer is for a full warranty. The law provides consumers protection by preventing a warranty being conditional upon receipt of a postcard. However, a limited warranty often must be registered, so those little self-addressed postcards can be important.

Keep all your paperwork, contracts, warranties and other documents together. All of the pieces are part of the same remodeling project. If you have a problem with either the contractor or a manufacturer, and you need legal assistance to get your problem solved or you want to act on your behalf in small claims court, you need documents in good order.

You can purchase home warranty policies that will protect the major components of a house. For example, a single-family house older than 10 years old, less than 4,000 square feet, located in a large city in the Midwest would cost about $439 per year. The items typically covered are:

- Central heating system
- Duct work
- Dishwasher
- Clothes washer
- Built-in microwave
- Plumbing pipe leaks
- Sump pump
- Jetted bath tubs
- Garbage disposal
- Electrical system
- Central vacuum
- Roof leaks
- Central air conditioning
- Kitchen refrigerator
- Oven / range /cooktop
- Clothes dryer
- Plumbing system
- Water heater
- Water softener
- Toilets
- Trash compactor
- Ceiling fans
- Garage door opener

Be assured that there are limits and deductibles and that this kind of insurance is not for everyone. See The Resources below.

The Resources

For more information about home warranty policies visit *www.AmericanHomeShield.com* or *www.warrantybynet.com.* Both these companies, and others, can provide additional warranty protection for a fee.

An excellent consumer reference book is the *American Bar Association Family Legal Guide, Third Edition* (American Bar Association, 2004). This and other useful books are available at *www.abanet.org.*

13

What If You Really Need to Make Changes?

The Challenge

For many people, projecting what is on paper or what is seen on a 3-D model is not easy. There is an element of risk–and an element of blind faith in your architect and contractor. You receive assurances that it will be just want you want and that the plan, when executed, will be functional, clean, bright and visually appealing. This experience is especially difficult if this is your first remodeling project. It is further complicated if more than one person is making the final decisions–partners often have dissimilar views or expectations, and interpret the plans differently.

It is possible that some part of the remodeling will not be completely satisfying. You get all or part of the way through the project, and you realize that the work, quality of materials or the general layout are not what you intended. Panic sets in as you come to grips with the fact that you possibly have to live with something that you do not want or like.

There is a difference between quality of execution and indifference to–or dislike of–the remodeling as specified. If the work is substandard, then the focus is on the contractor and subcontractors to redo the work or refund the money. However, if the work is done to specifications and you are still unhappy, you have to decide just how much it bothers you and what you can live with. Such decisions have serious financial realities. It will certainly mean that you will go over budget.

Of course, the further you are into the project, the more painful the tear-out of the new work is. It is one matter to rip up 20 tiles and return the unused portion to the store and choose another pattern. It is an entirely different matter to realize that the room configuration is wrong or that the installed cabinets are the wrong style or color and must come out. Change-outs, other than contractor failure to perform, are very expensive–any changes in structural work make it even more costly.

The Facts

Part of the problem that homeowners face when remodeling is the sheer number of products available on the market. Take a simple item like door hinges and pulls for kitchen cabinets: a major home improvement center offered 16 styles in stock, with the option of looking through catalogs at hundreds more. It is easy to make a mistake.

Education is the key to not being a victim of your own whims. One store manager confessed that when homeowners see displays in the store, they respond enthusiastically to the quality, color or choice of materials but they cannot or do not try to understand how it will look in their homes.

There can be subtle and not-so-subtle pressures during remodeling. Family members, guests and even the contractor himself might suggest that the wrong materials were chosen or the layout is not right. You are under pressure; you have time and financial constraints, and you have 10 minutes to decide whether it is right or not. If the sums are large, take your time. It is far better to manage the process professionally and without pressure or emotion, than to make a $10,000 snap decision.

If you decide to makes changes after the work is started (or completed), remember that not just labor costs are involved. There can also be hidden charges when returning materials and supplies to the store. For example, undamaged items can be returned for credit, but in some cases there may be a hefty restocking fee.

If you change your mind after the fact, the contractor is not responsible for the correction. You will absorb the entire cost of new cabinets, flooring, electrical work or painting. Accept that fact.

Some Websites offer contractors information on how to use change orders as a profit center, and there are some contractors who will manipulate the situation to generate higher fees and additional work. How often this happens is hard to say. Be particularly leery if, for example, the contractor offers to take the cabinets you decided to replace at the last minute off your hand for a few dollars.

At the time of the contract, you need to anticipate the possibility that changes will be made from the original specification. A *change order* is the document used by most contractors to specify, in writing, changes authorized by the homeowners. Under no circumstances should you approve even the smallest changes without a written authorization.

Contractors who are experienced (and honest) may actually be proactive about the use of change orders. They feel that it protects them as much as the homeowner. At times, it is the contractor who is the master of the budget, assigning specific costs to finishes and materials. While it may be hard to swallow, you benefit in the long run.

The contractor is not the only one with whom you should have written change orders. Draftsmen, architects and designers should be subject to the same discipline as your builder.

One interesting problem is if changes have to be made because of hidden defects in the house–internal damage from water or insects, stack pipes or water lines that were not anticipated, substandard work from the original builder or a remodeler in times past. Who pays for this kind of change–which can be very expensive? There is always a good-faith element in every remodeling project and that is the reason you budget for contingencies. But as a homeowner, these kinds of necessary alterations never make you feel better, especially when they result from *hidden* defects.

The Solutions

Make sure that your contractor does not underprice the bid and then come back to announce that it cannot be done because of a deficient building site or poor quality design. After-the-fact changes are a great way to improve contractor margins.

You will help your cause and save money if you can read the blueprints (if you cannot, ask for help–you paid for it). The tape measure is your best friend. Ensure that the work is being done to specifications. Recheck your color swatches, tiles samples and trim specifications. Learn the difference between poplar and common pine.

Make sure that any change orders include both materials and labor; in haste you may authorize improving the window trim without realizing that the custom work is going to cost 50 percent more in labor. It is very easy to overlook this cost, so ask your contractor to be specific about the full costs.

Before you authorize significant changes, go back to square one and make sure that the change order meets local codes and building requirements–otherwise you may have to approve a second change order for the same work. Ask your contractor for advice about products or remodeling changes where budgets can be scaled back to compensate for changes you would like to make.

Carefully examine any statements from a contractor who tells you that agreed-upon materials are not available or additional labor is needed. The contractor may be trying to get you to commit unnecessarily more money for both materials and labor, thus potentially increasing his or her profit margins.

If you must change out what is already done, see if you can live with compromises. Can you strip or stain cabinets rather than rip them out and buy another set of cabinets? The same is true with flooring, wall colors, wallpaper and trim around windows and doors. Can you make superficial changes to the adjoining rooms so that everything looks more connected? Perhaps you can rearrange the furniture or decorations to enhance part of the space you like and take attention away from the so-called defects.

If you end up with materials that are useable but cannot be returned, you can always try to recover some money by selling them on the Web or at a garage sale, by selling them to your contractor or by giving them away to a not-for-profit foundation which buys building materials to fund low-cost housing (and take a tax deduction in the process).

The Resources

One of the least expensive legal forms providers online offers a simple change order for $2.99 as a download to your computer. Visit *www.e-formsonline.com* for details. Like many of the online forms provider, once you buy this form, you have access to it for future use.

14

Remodeling from the Contractor's Point of View

The Challenge

Much has been said here and elsewhere about the importance of finding the right contractor, making sure that the contract is specific and that you are familiar with and understand the remodeling process you are about to begin. Seemingly, the burden of proof is always on the contractor; rarely do you hear from the contractors, architects, sub-contractors or designers who work for clients with unrealistic expectations and even more unrealistic budgets

However, can you imagine what it is like to be the contractor on most remodeling projects? There are some homeowners who simply have one point of view: they want their job finished on time, on budget and as specified. They do not care how it will get done, whether the contractor has a fair deal or, if problems occur, how they can work together to solve the problems.

Obviously, not every client is like this. Most people, in the spirit of what they are intending to accomplish with their remodeling project, are enthusiastic and positive and will work with the contractor or architect to reach their mutual goals. But even with the best of intentions, the situation can become tense—nerves are frayed and everyone loses patience from time to time.

Assuming that the working relationship begins in a friendly, but business-like manner, the goal is to maintain that spirit of cooperation. The greatest challenge is to maintain your cool in the light of increasing expenditures or when the job gets hopelessly behind, no matter whose fault it is.

The Facts

Your contractor is part of a business process. His or her work has been researched, interviewed, questioned and examined. He is often asked to provide financial information about his privately held business.

Contracting is a very competitive business. New people, qualified or not, enter the remodeling business all the time and the best way to get established is to complete on price. They do not have a list of previous jobs to show, nor can they necessarily compete on the extras contractors often provide: design, material and construction suggestions that may improve a renovation or keep costs in line.

As small business people, they have to make a profit, keep employees, schedule jobs, find good subcontractors and buy supplies and materials at the best prices. Further, it is easy to make mistakes in bidding for a job, and unless the homeowner is in a generous mood, the contractor will eat most of the error.

Also, contractors do have personal lives outside of their businesses. They appreciate a phone call at 10 p.m. no more than you would. Contractors report regularly that there is a tendency on the part of homeowners to hear only what they want to hear: the price and delivery date. They are often frustrated by homeowners' inability or unwillingness to grasp the whole picture.

Most contractors want and need you to be organized and detailed. It ensures that everyone is on the same page. Further, they want you to learn something about the construction business and they want you to understand the terms and the order of work they do—it makes their job is much easier. They also want you to know that you are probably not their only client and that they will not be on site every day.

Like everyone else, your contractor wants to have rational conversations with rational people. If you can hold the line on your emotions, there is a good chance he will also. Remember, he has been through this before; this is not the first job he has ever done. He has seen unexpected problems, experienced delays in schedules because of subcontractors or material delays, and he does not have the same emotional (or financial) investment in the renovation.

As you work with this individual, it is worth thinking about exactly what the contractor/homeowner relationship is. Your contractor…

- …is not your new best friend.
- …is not your designer or architect, unless you engaged him for those services from the beginning.
- …is not your financial adviser and should never be privy to your financial resources.
- …is not prepared or willing to make your decisions for you—you have to decide which shade of green works.
- …cannot be expected to pick up your part of the work.
- …is as much affected by delays as you are.
- …does not need you to tell him how to do his job or stand around and watch everything.

…is not a mind reader; he has expectations that your directions will be clear, concise and in writing.

…hates to hear the words–I want to make a few changes…

…has every right to charge for changes you decide to make.

…needs decisions on a timely basis. He cannot keep his schedule unless you do your part.

…is not a marriage counselor and should not be put in the middle when there are differences of opinion.

…expects payment as called for in the contract. If there are problems, you are certainly free to withhold some or all of the money until the matter is resolved.

…expects change orders in writing.

…would hope that if he does a good job, you would recommend him to friends and family and that such a recommendation would not be withheld unreasonably.

In one of your meetings with the contractor, you may hear the words *bid, estimate, proposal* or *contract*. They have different meanings, and it is essential that both parties agree as to what is meant:

- A bid is a conditional offer to do something, usually for a lump sum.
- An estimate is a judgment indicating the *likely* cost or range of costs for a job. It is not a firm price.
- A proposal is an offer that certain work will be done for a certain amount of money.
- The contract is the final, legally binding document that seals the deal.

A bid or estimate is usually followed by a proposal, which is then solidified by a contract. Your contractor may use one or all of these vehicles as part of his business.

Your contractor assumes that you will get more than one estimate for the work you want done. He also assumes that you are comparing apples with apples–that everyone bid on the same set of specifications. You may find yourself in an awkward situation if the contractor, after various meetings and discussions, does not want to do business with you. He or she may have too much work or does not feel qualified to do the project as you presented it.

For example, the contractor may be unfamiliar with parts of the work you require–very elaborate trim and molding work, perhaps. Some contractors avoid older homes because they assume there are hidden problem–structural, electrical or other setbacks that will interfere with smooth operations. Often contractors will pass on a job because it is too small–or too large.

The Solutions

First and foremost, deal in facts. Do not make wild statements or offer comments that are not true. It is unprofessional and motivates no one.

Know from the beginning that there are going to be some problems and work *with* the contractor. Try to understand their circumstances and problems with materials, schedules, laborers and the job's complexity.

For everyone's sake, put everything in writing. Keep your records up to date and make sure that the contractor has copies of all pertinent documents, such as change orders. Do not assume anything and do not expect your contractor to work for free. Do not borrow or use your contractor's tools, truck or equipment without his permission. People who own tools are very protective; besides they are expensive to replace.

The Resources

If you are interested in learning more about the construction business, visit a site like *www.constructionbusinessowner.com,* which is devoted exclusively to owners of construction companies. The issues and problems they are concerned about can be very informative, especially the legal and financial sides of the business. Once you understand a bit more about the costs of doing business, you will be able to rationalize the quotes you have received and understand why they are so high!

Tame Your Contractor: A Homeowner's Guide to Working with Contractors (Booklocker.com, 2004) gives you all the secrets of working with contractors from a 30-year veteran of the industry. Visit *www.booklocker.com* for this and other titles of interest.

15

Who Is the
Building Inspector and
Why Is He Here?

The Challenge

Because you own a home, it does not mean that you have the right to do with it what you want. All levels of government have put limits on property owners. Your challenge is to build, remodel or change your property to your wishes without being in violation of the law. At any stage of ownership, you will be required to be in accordance with certain standards established by government or local governing bodies such as homeowners associations and historical district boards. All three may have some authority over the use and physical appearance of your property. Property rights are not absolute rights, and some form of building inspection has been built into the system to ensure compliance.

Most people accept the right of local government to regulate renovations and remodeling. The nastiest fights tend to be between individual owners and homeowners associations or historical district governing boards. Many owners do not read or understand the covenants set by local boards and challenge the right of these boards to enforce their rules. Often the rules themselves are vague and subject to broad interpretation. There may be a rule against loud or unusual exterior colors on a home. People might agree that orange, pink or purple exteriors contravene such a rule. But does deep red also fall outside the guidelines? And who interprets the rules for enforcement? Your neighbor who happens to be on the local governing council?

Historical districts are often particularly strict when homeowners wish to renovate their homes. The resulting process can be very expensive and time-consuming. Recall a year-long episode of the television series *This Old House* that was staged in an historic district. There were very strict limitations imposed on the owners and the contractors as they worked to make a 250-year old house modern. Any changes to the façade, even the materials used, came under severe scrutiny. Everything had to be presented to the local governing council, and a great deal of money had to be spent on architectural drawings and sample materials before any real work was completed.

Within reason, contractors and homeowners make common cause in their desire to renovate a property quickly, cheaply and efficiently. Local government or governing bodies, through some kind of inspection process, are there to see that all building and remodeling activity is within a reasonable standard. (What is reasonable to the homeowners association and to the homeowner may be a matter for discussion.)

Before, during and after renovation, the one thing you wish to avoid is a problem with building inspectors. They have the authority to stop your work before it has begun—or at any time during construction. They can mandate that even completed work be removed and rebuilt at your expense. Cordial and professional relations with a building inspector are a must. Homeowners often try to start construction work without building permits and proper inspection. Just as frequently, neighbors and local officials ensure that work will not continue without the proper documents, drawings and permits.

The Facts

State government has the authority to pass legislation to protect the general well-being. These powers are, in turn, delegated to the county, township or city through *enabling legislation* which allows local government to zone land use, determine whether a building is safe and establish sanitary and noise conditions.

The first zoning laws and regulations were enacted in New York in 1916. These and similar laws were upheld by the Supreme Court in the 1920s. Such laws must be reasonable and not arbitrarily applied. They cannot be so restrictive as to violate basic property rights. For example, a building inspector cannot approve a 40' x 40' addition on one side of the street and disallow it on the other (all things being equal).

Zoning and subsequent inspection are often based on:

- The size of your lot.
- The kind of structure allowed in your area.
- Setbacks from the lot line (you cannot build right next to your neighbor's house).
- The height of the building.
- Density (a ratio between the amount of land and the structures).
- Appearance of the completed home.

There may be other issues, depending on the local governance.

The local zoning department issues a permit for property owners before they can begin any major renovation or rebuilding. The permit is typically based on preliminary drawings and a general indication that the renovation does not violate zoning laws for that area. If the planned improvements do not conform to local zoning laws, a variance can be allowed. In most cases, property owners will seek an *area variance*, meaning they seek an exception to setbacks, building heights, lot width or lot size. (This is opposed to a *use variance*, which applies to building a business in a residential area.)

Applying for a variance generally requires a public hearing, usually before a zoning appeals board. You may be awarded a variance if you can show that it will not adversely affect a neighboring property or go against the spirit of the zoning laws. While variances are often granted, they will not be allowed when the homeowner begins a renovation without the proper permits and applies for a variances after the fact. This is called a *self-created hardship*. Ignorance of the law cannot be used as an excuse.

Some homeowners can be rather casual about building permits and inspectors. You may suffer adverse consequences as a result of ignorance of zoning law or your willingness to take your chances with the neighbors or zoning board. And do not think that just because you have finished building something, the inspector would never make you take it down.

In the extreme, there can be criminal penalties, though civil penalties usually apply. You may get a cease and desist order, stopping further construction, or you may be asked to remove what has been built. In addition, the municipality might refuse further permits, perhaps leaving your renovation half-built. Incomplete work can also adversely affect the value of your property.

The Solutions

Interview your prospective contractor carefully about his or her knowledge of the zoning and permitting process. Problems with the building inspector and the zoning board are one of the main reasons you hired a contractor and architect in the first place. They must advise you as to the process, including costs. If the contractor asks you to get permits, find another contractor.

Research and know the law. This is especially important if you are serving as your own general contractor. Almost every municipality posts requirements for zoning on its municipal Website (see The Resources at the end of this chapter).

Interview a building inspector to find out the most common problems. Your compliance serves their purposes as well as yours. You can also hire a building consultant who is familiar with your local zoning codes. This is expensive, and would be necessary for only very large renovations projects.

If you get an order from the city to stop the work immediately, *stop the work immediately*. Show good faith and ask for help and direction. Ignoring cease and desist orders accomplishes nothing. Make direct contact with your contractor and the building inspector. Get the details in writing and identify what specific problems need to be resolved and by when. If your contractor and architect have specified work that is not code, you have remedies. It is their responsibility to build according to local specifications. Insist that they resolve the matter at their cost, not yours. Consider firing your contractor immediately, but do not lose contact with him or her in case there are further problems and costs.

Some municipalities have a program of *self-certification*, whereby a qualified and trained architect takes the place of a city inspector. Doing this could save you a great deal of time and money. (Note that contractors are not self-certified.)

The Resources

There are many sources, including local municipal Websites, of building code information. Visit *www.findlaw.com/11strategy/* for local zoning codes. It will take some work to find your way through the vast amount of information. Another site to visit is *www.local.com*. You will be able to find the city of your choice, including many smaller municipalities located around major cities.

16

Do You Need
a Lawyer?

The Challenge

When renovating, it is important to figure out whether you need legal advice, how much help you need and how much you can afford to pay.

Is this book anti-lawyer? No. Is this book anti-extra expense? Yes. And with lawyers, it is not just the expense that comes into play–it is also the delays. Just because you have hired a lawyer, do not assume that he or she is sitting by the phone waiting to hear from you. You are one of maybe hundreds of clients. What is more, the size of your expected fee may have a direct influence on your lawyer's priorities: your 2 hours of work may not compare favorably with that of a long-standing client who each month buys 20 hours of your lawyer's time at a higher rate.

Decide whether you can do some or all of your own legal work. Your challenge is not to avoid lawyers completely, but to use legal advice cost-effectively. If your project is reasonably small, consider writing up a simple contract. If you have problems with a subcontractor, write a strong letter instead of running to a lawyer. As a general rule, the more costly the renovation is, the greater the need to protect your assets and get *some* legal representation.

If the cost of the renovation is the gauge of legal necessity, put yourself in the situation of the homeowner who has hired a contractor to remodel a small bathroom for a fee of $2,500. Work was begun and then came to a halt as the contractor figured out that a larger, much more lucrative project needed his or her attention. Fortunately, the homeowner followed good advice and did not pay beyond the work completed.

The homeowner threatened to sue for breach of contract. The contractor was unfazed and refused to complete the work. The remaining portion of the job, estimated to be worth about $1,000, could be completed by the homeowner, a handyman or another contractor. Rushing to a lawyer would serve little purpose.

The initial contact with a lawyer and a simple letter to the contractor would cost around $350. If the contractor goes back and finishes the job, completing the project now costs $1,350.

In this case, it would be better to cut your losses and get the work done. Even if you win, it could take months to get the matter settled (during which time you would have no bathroom).

The Facts

An informal survey of lawyers in the Midwest suggests that the hourly rates for legal advice range from $100 per hour (not typical) to more than $400 per hour. The cost of a lawyer for both the initial contract phase and any potential conflicts post construction must be added to the budget. If you use a lawyer, you need some kind of document to outline your agreement with the lawyer (a contract before the contract). This is often called a retainer agreement or representation agreement. It puts in writing the lawyer's fees and identifies who will work on the case.

Finding the right lawyer is much like finding the right contractor. Not all lawyers handle contracts or real estate matters. Check with family, friends, neighbors, co-workers or professional associations that can provide referrals (see The Resources at the end of this chapter).

While the fee is not everything, it certainly matters a lot. Because there is no such thing as a standard fee structure, you can negotiate an hourly rate. And be warned–a low fee does not necessarily mean money well spent. A novice may end up billing three times the hours and cost more than an experienced lawyer who would need far less time even at a higher rate.

Many basic legal agreements, like construction contracts, are boilerplate that lawyers buy from legal publishers. These documents require little revision or specialized work. The only real wordsmithing is customizing the document to fit your circumstances–work that will probably be done by a legal assistant or paralegal. And then? Then you get a $450 bill for 2 hours of legal work. This figure alone should have you asking why you could not just compose a basic document yourself (see The Resources at the end of this chapter).

If matters come to a head, and there is a serious dispute over the contract, your lawyer will ask you to be an active participant. Write down all the details and a summary of events leading up to the problem with the contractor. A timeline, or a simple dated sequence of events, is a big help. It must be accurate, as your claim is based on these facts. Do not embellish and do not lie.

The Solutions

Decide the value of your project in relation to your income and resources. A renovation costing $200,000 needs all the protection you can muster, no matter the size of your income. If the remodeling costs are $5,000, say, you will probably not need legal assistance to get a good, working agreement.

You can cut your legal costs by grouping your renovation questions with other areas such as your will, estate planning or legal advice for your business. You are going to be charged for an hour anyway, so get a full hour's worth.

Also, play an active part. Gather documents, do some of the typing and proofreading or even write up the first draft yourself using generic legal documents that you can buy online. Learn as much as you can about contract law and how to handle construction or renovation disputes. The more you know, the less you will have to pay in billable hours.

Some sources suggest that you can do the work yourself and hire the lawyer as a coach, teaching you the law and suggesting ways to accomplish your objectives. Generally, this is not a realistic option. Lawyers are not eager to assist do-it-yourselfers in the practice of the law. One reason is that lawyers still retain liability even if they participate in the legal process indirectly.

Instead of hiring a lawyer or doing it yourself, you might consider using non-lawyer professionals, including paralegals. For a basic contract, the cost would be substantially lower. If disputes arise however, the paralegal would not have sufficient training to handle problems.

Act on problems at the first sign of real difficulty, especially if there is a lot of money involved. Obviously, you cannot afford to pick up the phone and talk with your attorney every time some little issue arises, but do not let problems get out of hand without advice and support.

Should a dispute occur, you must be organized. Have all the necessary documents and information, including canceled checks, existing contracts, letters, copies of faxes and e-mails with the contractor or other disputing party. Respond as quickly as you can for requests for information. Make sure your attorney knows your schedule and where you can be contacted at all times.

The issues of good communication with your lawyer are the same as those discussed in Chapter 9: *Communication Is the Key*, which addressed good communication with your contractor. Set the tone of the working relationship at the first meeting. Make sure that it is clear that you are in charge. In addition, a good client-attorney relationship will be maintained if your lawyer takes the time to explain your case, the cost-effectiveness of various strategies, and any risks involved.

Make sure that you are a good client. Follow through on what you promise. Tell your lawyer everything, knowing that he or she must keep what you have to say confidential. Respect your attorney's time and schedule. You have only a reasonable claim on his or her time. Also, have the decency to pay your bill on time.

The Resources

The American Bar Association, and local and state bar associations, maintain databases and will provide you will a list of referrals from which to choose a competent attorney. They will not recommend a lawyer. Visit *www.aba.org* for more details. After choosing a lawyer, you can learn more about his or her background by visiting *www.martindale.com,* which contains biographical sketches of many practicing attorneys.

There are many fine legal sites for the do-it-yourselfer that supply not only legal forms but also a good deal of information. Visit *www.socrates.com, www.nolo.com* and *www.findlaw.com.*

17

Arbitration:
Beats a Lawsuit
Every Time

The Challenge

No one wants to admit that a renovation might not go as planned. You prefer not to believe that we could ever be in conflict with an architect, contractor or specialty supplier. But you must consider this possibility when starting renovation.

So, why might matters not go as expected? The first big culprit is bad communication. The second is a failure to manage expectations–on your part and the contractor's. And the results of such failures? Seemingly endless delays, cost over-runs, undocumented changes or conversations–*he said, she said*–and much more.

There is a good chance that much of this can be prevented. Record every conversation, change order, decision, specification, budgeted item, cost over-run, e-mail and letter. Leave nothing to chance and nothing to memory. Pull out the digital camera and record progress–or lack of it. There is a date stamping with each image and they can be stored electronically, so there's no need to print them until you need to. And beware: the longer and larger the renovation, the harder it is to assemble the facts.

There is a case for resolving conflict simply by paying more. Money often makes problems go away. You can compromise on schedules and the quality of materials, each party agreeing to split the difference. This of course assumes that you are still on speaking terms and that the money involved and/or the compromises are tolerable, which is not always the case.

If compromise does not work (and it must be documented), then you can sue, using mediation or arbitration. Arbitration is increasingly part of any business contract or agreement. However, there is one situation where court is the only option–the presence of fraud. In such circumstances, sue the other party and take no prisoners. You help everyone by getting thieves out of the construction business.

The Facts

We live in very litigious society. There are tens of thousands of lawyers eager to accept an hourly rate of $200 to $300 (or more) to punish your contractor. But is revenge what you really want? Will getting even get the rest of the kitchen remodeled and livable?

Small claims court is often an effective remedy in some cases, generally involving sums less than $5,000, although each state may set individual limits. The cost to file varies, but is typically around $50. The small claims court is a *pro se* court, meaning that you act on your own behalf. Lawyers are not allowed to represent you in court, though you are certainly free to consult an attorney beforehand. Physical evidence and records are the keys to success. Decisions are often rendered within 30 days and can be appealed, though there are time limits for appeals.

No appetite for courtrooms? Consider invoking the mediation or arbitration clauses that are a part of a quality contract. Consumers often confuse the two, but there is a great deal of difference.

Let us start with mediation, which is often simply a form of fee-based negotiation. A mediator is not necessarily a lawyer; in fact, he or she does not give legal advice as part of the process. Mediation attempts to establish a meeting of minds, allowing both parties to discuss their grievances and settle the dispute in an informal, non-binding way. The mediator simply facilitates an objective discussion of the situation.

Mediation often works, but can be expensive–perhaps $100 or more per hour. A full day's session could reach $1,000 and the two parties still might not agree to settle. The fee is usually paid by the party requesting mediation; if a court orders mediation, then both parties split the bill. A good mediator is active in the process, trying to persuade each party to compromise and come to an agreement. Either party can have an attorney present. If an agreement is reached, it is wise to have a document prepared immediately as an addendum to a contract and to have the solution recorded.

Arbitration has increasingly become the means for settling disputes, as it offers a lower-cost method of getting matters settled. An arbitrator is like a judge, gathering the facts and issuing a decision. He or she decides the matter based on the merits of the case, and does not try to reach consensus. The arbitrator's decision is final– both parties are bound to the decision and cannot, as a rule, go to court.

Some local business bureaus offer arbitration services, often at little cost. Volunteer members agree to serve and settle disputes. However, the decision is still final and binding on both parties.

The Solutions

Your contract should allow for some kind of dispute resolution other than civil action; clauses for either mediation or arbitration or both are standard, no matter who prepares the document. Make sure that such contingencies are included in the contract. Check the language about conflict resolution carefully; if arbitration is given as an option, the right to sue, even in small claims court, is often waived. Make sure that is what you want.

Should mediation not work, arbitration can be the next step (if your contract allows for it). Both processes can take place in person, on the phone or by video-conferencing. In desktop arbitration, disputes are resolved solely on written statements presented to the arbitrator.

When giving notice of arbitration, make sure that it is in writing. Ensure that it is sent by certified mail so you get confirmation that notice has been received. Give a copy to your lawyer. Do not rely on e-mail or any means of communication where you cannot document the notice.

Arbitrators themselves are often lawyers who either volunteer their time or are paid for their services. Insist on an arbitrator who knows something about the construction industry. Impartiality is paramount—find out what other cases he or she has worked on, as well as their training, education and length of time as an arbitrator (or mediator). If you work through an organization like the Better Business Bureau, you may not have much say in who your arbitrator is.

When preparing your case for the arbitrator, ask questions about the process and follow the rules. File your claim early. If you delay, you might forget details and lose those all-important documents. If you intend to have witnesses (assuming this is allowed), get their statements in writing.

Remember the evidence: nothing speaks louder than pictures, paperwork, e-mail and letters. This is crucial.

Finally, arbitration is binding: awards made by a private judge or arbitrator as part of a valid contract (assuming fraud is not in evidence) are enforced by state and federal courts.

The Resources

The basic resources for mediation and arbitration are local. They are often free or have limited fees. As mentioned, the local Better Business Bureau is a great place to start. Also consider the local bar association or law schools in your area. Canvas the Internet for your state attorney general's office or local consumer affairs offices (many large cities have them).

The federal government comes down hard on fraud and businesses that appear to rip off consumers. The Federal Trade Commission (FTC) at *www.ftc.gov* offers consumers a lot of information and resources. Take the time to look and learn about alternative dispute resolution (ADR).

The FTC site makes specific mention of the Association of Conflict Resolution as an example of a privately-run service that may be a substantial resource. Visit *www.ACRnet.org.*

The American Arbitration Association has an extensive Website to examine at *www.adr.org.* Be careful when looking at related sites, because many of them serve the construction industry, not consumers.

Sites like *www.arbitrator.com* and *www.privatejudge.com* are interesting and informative, the latter offering a for-fee service for conflict resolution and arbitration.

And remember: you do not have to go it alone. Your personal attorney can be a huge help. There are times when a strongly worded letter–with an impressive letterhead–can do the trick.

18

General Health and Safety on the Job Site

The Challenge

Any home renovation involving more than a few rooms is a major health and safety issue. Chapter 23: *Should You Live In or Move Out During Construction?* addresses the issues about remaining or moving out during construction.

It would be inexcuseable for your family or workers to be hurt during renovation when it could easily have been prevented. Job safety is not easy, especially if your renovation is major. You would assume that the contractor or sub-contractors would be as interested and concerned about safety as you are, but it is very easy to cut corners:

- Ladders are used instead of scaffolding.
- Tools and materials are left out overnight.
- Large and heavy objects are moved without sufficient workers.
- Shortcuts are taken on temporary stairs between floors.
- The worksite is poorly maintained, with debris everywhere.
- Outside work is conducted in hazardous weather.

Determine at the outset who is primarily responsible for safety and maintaining the work environment. This should be discussed with your contractor before a contract is signed and work has begun. Agree on any division of responsibilities; put it in writing and make sure that the standard is met daily.

If the construction work is substantial, safety issues extend to neighbors, and even to the inspectors who come onto your property. If work or materials extend beyond your property lines, ensure the safety and well-being of neighboring persons and property. You must have your neighbor's permission to go onto his or her property, even for a short period of time. Also, problems like noise and fumes may become an issue. You cannot contain them in any reasonable way, though you can be sensitive and communicate with neighbors.

If you need to stage work for the duration of the project, get written permission allowing for this kind of easement. Naturally, you and your insurance (or perhaps your contractor and his or her insurance) will be responsible for any damage.

The Facts

Your construction site is an *attractive nuisance*, both legally and practically. To understand the concept of an attractive nuisance, think of people who have in-ground swimming pools. The law puts the burden on them to secure the site, because it is almost impossible for children to resist the urge for a quick dip. If you own it and if you maintain it, you are responsible for accidents and problems that may occur.

But there is more to the issue than just the site. The materials, the workers and the work itself pose risks to persons and property. Consider the following:

- Ladders not balanced, extended too far, not secured to the structure or left up when not in use.
- Solvents and paint thinners are a hazard, certainly if ingested, but also if spilled on finished surfaces or the skin.
- Lead paint is a very important issue for older homes. If your house was built before 1978, it may pose a much higher risk of lead exposure. Lead is toxic for all ages, not just children.
- Excessive exposure to radon is a problem. Torn up basement floors could expose the home to large doses.
- Asbestos is found in the most basic products, from floor and ceiling tiles to insulation around furnaces and pipes. Homes built before 1980 are more likely to have asbestos. All forms of asbestos are dangerous, because the fibers are so small and can get trapped in the lungs.
- Tools, especially pneumatic nailers and electric saws pose real threats for the untrained.
- Objects stacked too high, tools or material placed on upper ledges–in short, falling objects of any kind–pose a risk to the unsuspecting.
- Temporary walls or half-walls that are not properly secured.
- Areas open to the elements (rain and snow make work surfaces slippery).
- Sustained periods of loud noise without proper protection (this can cause hearing loss). Noise is measured in decibels and is recorded on a scale such that 73 decibels is twice as loud as 70 (normal talking). A jackhammer is 102 to 111 decibels; a portable saw 80-100 decibels. Everyone (not just workers) exposed to these levels of noise can suffer hearing loss.
- Unvented propane heaters–a risk for both fire and inhalation of fumes.
- Mold and mildew are another health risk. They grow best in warm, humid, damp conditions.

- Carbon monoxide poisoning from temporarily rigged heaters poses substantial danger, as it is colorless and nearly odorless.

The Solutions

Your first task when renovating a home is to protect yourself by protecting others. Secure the work area. If the work includes construction beyond the original footprint of the house, secure the site with temporary fencing of sufficient quality and height. Waist-high orange tape or plastic fencing will not do. Your fencing should be locked and the site should be lit at night. Ensure that this cost is part of the contract in the first place. It should not be your responsibility to pay more for this basic security.

In changing neighborhoods and for very large renovations, you may consider hiring a security service–at least one that drives by and checks the premises when work is not in progress. Thieves can remove expensive materials and sell them quickly and easily. Arson, too, is a real possibility. In any case, if the work being done is substantial, you may want to have builders risk insurance, which would cover the cost of labor and material already used.

Again, you need to see a certificate of insurance, including workman's compensation. Also, as part of the contractor's general liability insurance, there should be completed operations coverage, guaranteeing the contractor's ability to do the work.

Additional insurance over and above your contractor's is a must. We live in a very litigious society and lawsuits for substantial money damages are common. A change to your homeowner's policy is probably the easiest and cheapest way to manage this. Talk to your insurance agent.

If you have taken on additional insurance, consider assuming some of the health and safety risk yourself by increasing the size of your deductible. A normal deductible could be $500 or so. Increase it to $2,500, for example, and you could save quite a bit. Make sure that this amount is part of your renovation budget.

Even if you do not agree to be part of the clean-up and safety crew, you need to inspect the site daily to ensure that reasonable standards are maintained. But remember, renovation sites are inherently messy: insisting that the area be broom cleaned each night is reasonable; insisting that it be perfect is not. Review what hazards need correcting and take action.

Post the telephone numbers for the fire and emergency ambulance service in your area. Post them for everyone to see. Keep an emergency medical kit in the work area. Also, add additional smoke, carbon monoxide and radon detectors in the house and worksite. They are inexpensive protection.

Insist that loud construction equipment be maintained properly with new mufflers. Generators and compressors should be placed as far away as possible from the renovation site/home. Ask the contractor to rotate noisy jobs with quieter jobs. If necessary, consider wearing hearing protection if you are on the job site for an extended period of time.

If you suspect asbestos, OSHA requires that your contractor act as though it were there. That means using a specialized service with approved equipment and procedures to remove it from the site. If there is asbestos on the site and it is not disturbed (not breaking apart, for example) you do not need to remove it. Your responsibility is to secure it by painting, covering or wrapping the affected area.

If you have had a problem with mold in the past, your renovation is the perfect time to correct the problem. Proper venting, replacement of moldy surfaces, removing moisture and even cleaning with a simple solution of one cup of bleach to one gallon of water will do the trick. Ensure that insulation is installed properly and that vents in crawl spaces and attics are included in your renovation plans. Make certain that the bathroom fan is adequate for the size of the room and is vented outside the house.

Test for the presence of lead paint. If present, it needs to be stabilized or removed, depending on local ordinances. As a rule, insist that it be removed rather than stabilized.

The Resources

Familiarize yourself with some of the basic OSHA safety rules as a means to monitoring your contractor's working conditions. Visit *www.osha.gov* for more details.

19

Being Your Own General Contractor: The Pros and Cons

The Challenge

Consider the possibility of being your own general contractor (the individual you hire to manage the entire renovation process). At first blush, this strategy may sound bizarre, but in the right circumstances it can save a good deal of money and allows you to control the process according to your schedule and your ability to pay. Obviously, it is not for everyone. Perhaps a self-test is order:

Answer each of the following questions:

You are not a first-time homeowner.	yes/no
You have been involved in at least two prior renovation projects.	yes/no
You have a relative or friend in the building trades.	yes/no
You do not travel frequently for work.	yes/no
Your spouse is willing to assist with the management of the work.	yes/no
You have project management experience (work or volunteer).	yes/no
You are familiar with the individual trades (plumbing, roofing).	yes/no
Your renovation plans are not complicated or lengthy.	yes/no
You are willing to take moderate risks.	yes/no
You or your spouse are good at details.	yes/no
You or your partner can read and understand architect's drawings.	yes/no
You have no major family commitments (small children, aging parents).	yes/no
You do not attend school in the evenings.	yes/no

If you can answer *yes* to most of these, you are a candidate to be your own general contractor.

You now need to assess how complicated your renovations plans are. For example, the following are reasonable projects to manage:

- Bathroom improvements–new flooring, fixtures and decorating.
- Simple renovation of an existing kitchen–new flooring, cabinets and appliances.
- New deck or patio.
- Improvements to the family room–adding a fireplace, hardwood floors.
- Outdoor living space–including fencing, stonework and cooking area.
- Basement renovation–new interior walls, insulation, flooring and built-ins.

You will need professional management of the project if the work requires extensive new space such as a two-story addition, enlargement of kitchen and family rooms or the restructuring of attic space. Further, if your plans call for work that requires exceptions in the permitting process, a general contractor is essential. Likewise, if you attend school in the evening or have small children, aging parents or commitments outside work, use a general contractor.

The Facts

As a general guideline, being your own general contractor could save you as much as 25 percent of the total costs of a renovation project. You will not have to pay for:

- Liability insurance.
- General overhead, including marketing, office space, office help and utilities.
- Thirty percent markup on materials.
- Contractor's profit, perhaps as high as 10 percent.
- Fifteen percent markup on subcontractor's labor.

Being your own general contractor is *not* the same as doing the work yourself (see Chapter 8: *Finding a Contractor: Better Than Doing It Yourself*). Each role requires different skill sets with different time and work requirements. Of course, you may be able to do both: personally doing some of the work while acting as a general contractor.

Now consider what you *do not* get when you act as your own general contractor:

- Experienced advice.
- Qualified pools of specialty workers.
- Assistance with permits and inspectors.
- Quicker completion date (probably).
- A warranty on work completed.

As a general contractor, you need to be careful about risk management, specifically the possibility that someone might be hurt on the job and sue. It is doubtful that you can find construction insurance as a homeowner, but you can take on additional liability insurance–it is relatively cheap if you have a homeowner's policy. Do not be stingy: add $500,000 or more for the term of your renovation.

Further, if you are hiring workers as individuals (not for an incorporated company), you need to issue *Form 1099* to report the individual's income to the IRS. You will need the Social Security Number or Tax Identification Number for each worker. Also, you must file the *Annual Summary and Transmittal of U.S. Information Returns, Form 1096*, with the federal government. If you are unclear about these requirements, ask your accountant for assistance.

Your best bet is to hire subcontractors that are incorporated and have tax identification numbers from the federal government. Such companies are responsible for reporting their profits as well as tax deductions for their employees. Whether individuals or companies, subcontractors may pressure you to pay them in cash. Resist the pressure. You have no record of payment and it may be against the law. Pay for all materials and labor with a check. In case of dispute, proof of payment is absolutely essential.

The Solutions

If you choose to be actively involved as a general contractor, there are certain must-knows.

Familiarize yourself with the language of contracting, or at the very least expand your vocabulary. Bookstores and libraries are full of DIY books that explain basic and advanced projects. Tradespeople will have much greater respect for you and you will have less chance of being cheated if you know what you are talking about.

Home improvement stores are ideal environments to learn terms, procedures and more. In addition, they can provide the qualified labor and materials for your job (see Chapter 27: *Using the Big Box Building Center to Your Best Advantage*). Visit their Websites and you will see that they can handle almost any specific set of tasks. As general contractor, you can specify the materials and set the order. In effect, their workers become your subcontractors.

Learn the order of the work to be done (assuming no structural or foundation work):

- Demolition. Turn off electricity and water in the work area.
- Roughing in with framing carpenters, making sure that the roof, house wrap and windows are watertight. If you need roofing done, this is the time–moisture is your worst enemy.
- Plumbers and electricians generally arrive to rough in pipes and conduits.
- Installation of insulation, dry wall and tapers.

- Rooms are primed and painted.
- Installation of cabinets, built-ins, and flooring, finish carpentry are generally next in line.
- Fixtures are plumbed in.
- Electrical outlets and fixtures are wired and hung.
- You will probably have the painters back to stain woodwork and touch up the paint or add wallpaper.

Learn the permit process. It may require several visits to city offices to get the process right. Pay particular attention to the details and have your checkbook ready. You may not know this process and do not have the experience to walk your permit application through city or county government expeditiously.

Create a checklist that allows you to add schedule dates and completion dates as well as the amount paid to each subcontractor. A simple spreadsheet will do nicely. Leave room for notes and issues that may come up. Further, build a punch list as the work progresses. There are often dozens of small items that need attention. A cracked tile, damaged wall board, dirt on painted surfaces, fixtures hung in the wrong place—all of these may require that tradespeople come back and make adjustments. This is reason enough not to pay the full amount due until you are satisfied with the work. If you pay in full beforehand, you will not get the workers back easily.

Another possibility is to hire a contractor as a consultant, perhaps someone who is retired or semi-retired. Set a fixed-fee contract for this assistance. Decide how many hours you would need at an agreed-upon rate, always in writing. Reserve the option to buy additional time, if necessary. Agree the best time to talk and meet with your advisor. Your consultant may be a great source for qualified subcontractors. Do not be afraid to ask. If a serious problem arises, get your advisor on the job site for part of a day to manage the subcontractor problem.

The best advice is to treat your subcontractors with respect and patience. Write all instructions and changes in a log book for each tradesperson to view each day. Try to be there when they start or end the day. Give them your cell number so they can call if there are questions.

The Resources

For assistance on your responsibilities as an employer concerning wages, deductions and FICA collections, visit *www.irs.gov*.

For an excellent online glossary of construction terms, visit *www.soundhome.com*. There are even pictures and diagrams to further understanding. Visit *www.improvenet.com* where you will find a number of useful, free forms such as change orders and a punch list.

20

Should You Do the Renovation Yourself?

The Challenge

The world is filled with do-it-yourself (DIY) renovators—some good, some bad, most in between. The main reason for doing the work yourself is money. Labor is at least 50 percent of all home renovations projects, so thousands can be saved over the total life of the renovation. Of course, the extent of the renovation is a major factor in determining your ability and willingness to take on the work.

There are other motivations besides money. Some homeowners are hooked on historical preservation and carving their own space from an otherwise derelict or underused building. These are the brain and brawn behind the success stories in many cities where run-down areas are turned into trendy neighborhoods. There can also be huge financial rewards if the purchase and repair are *flipped* as the area improves and property values soar.

Are you a candidate for DIY? Consider the following:

- Do you like physical labor?
- Are you willing to get dirty?
- Do you finding projects frustrating or satisfying?
- Are there people you can turn to for advice and occasional help?
- Is your spouse in agreement?
- Can you isolate the workspace, knowing that it will take longer to finish?
- Can you admit when you cannot do certain things?
- Do you tend to procrastinate?
- Can you pick up a project after days or even weeks of delay?
- Are you willing to step aside once in a while in order to manage personal and business commitments?

There is a good deal more to DIY home renovation than the actual work. Remember that you are now the general contractor as well, so you have full responsibility for budgeting, quality control, permits, inspection, liability, safety, project management and scheduling. The variables grow geometrically in proportion to the size of the renovation project.

The Facts

The time needed to complete a renovation will double, triple or even quadruple depending on your motivation and commitment. Because you are probably not a skilled tradesman, you will possibly (probably) have to do work over, wasting time and materials. The old axiom–*Measure twice, cut once*–is ignored when you are tired or in a hurry to finish part of the renovation.

Be realistic about what you can and cannot do. Most people should not take on structural work, electric, plumbing or heating/air-conditioning renovation, except for the most basic work. Remember that you want your new space not only to look good, but to be safe. Both the quantity and quality of renovation will affect the eventual sales price of your home. Future buyers would be much more comfortable if they knew that sophisticated work was completed by specialists.

Think about how inconvenienced your family will be throughout any construction project, but particularly a do-it-yourself effort that will last more than a weekend or two. Everyone involved gets tired of the disruption.

Consider the neighbors as well. Perfectly nice, patient people get tired of looking over the fence at debris, lumber and construction equipment. Your eagerness to start early on Saturday with the power tools may not be compatible with their desire to sleep in. The trick is to make the neighbors your allies, not your enemies. That may mean a little extra effort, communicating your plans, apologizing for delays or the unsightly appearance and try to go out of your way to be sensitive. Avoid problems before they start.

You need to expect the same discipline of yourself as you would of a contractor. So if you decide to do it yourself, then every time you see the word *contractor* in this book, substitute your name. You have to put yourself on a budget, on a schedule, communicate to family and neighbors and so on.

You will occasionally need to ask friends or relatives for assistance. Be careful–dipping into this well too often will cause hard feelings. When asking for assistance, be specific and set a time convenient for your helpers. This may mean that a weekend or two passes before you can get the next phase of construction completed. People are generous and gracious, but if you ask them to do the dirty work or work a full weekend (or even a full day), you may be asking too much. Reward them with frequent breaks, pizza and cold drinks. Offer to reciprocate, knowing everyone who owns a home always has a list of projects. Do not take your partner's participation for granted, either. He or she may not have been keen to do without the services of a contractor in the first place.

The Solutions

If you are going to take on a renovation project yourself, personal discipline is crucial. A good rule of thumb is that some work has to be completed every day, no matter how tired you are. Some nights after work, you have energy and enthusiasm and can work 2 or 3 hours. Other nights, even weekends, 20 minutes of trash removal or stripping woodwork is all that you can do. But do at least one task of a project every day.

Buying and managing materials can take up an inordinate amount of time. Plan and write out your building materials and supplies needs and try to buy more than one day's requirement. Otherwise, you will spend more time coming and going from the building supply store than working on your renovation. You need to plan how and where you will store materials. Fifty 2 x 4s will not fit into the hall closet and they pose a danger if not stored properly. Designate an area–perhaps the garage, back porch or basement–as your staging area. Organize materials by order of the project. Label boxes and materials by color, location for use, when needed, etc. Keep a spreadsheet on materials purchased and the costs. This will help you keep your budget in line and your supplies available as needed.

Home centers and specialty stores rent almost every kind of construction equipment, from augers to compressors. Never buy a tool or equipment that you will use only once or twice. Call at least a week ahead of time and get a reservation (rental stores will often deliver and pick up the equipment). And consider avoiding the cost of rental entirely by asking friends and neighbors if you can borrow a specialty tool, remembering that you are responsible for maintenance and replacement, if necessary.

In addition to eventually enjoying your renovation, your first and most important goal is to pass the inspection stage. Know what is required. Ask questions, review the building codes, talk to inspectors–do everything possible to prepare for this process. If you fail to pass inspection, the costs and delays will compound.

Have a back-up plan if you get into trouble. In theory you are saving quite a bit, so do not be cheap at the wrong time. If you have to call in an experienced tradesman to complete part of the project, do so sooner than later (your budget should have a contingency amount in the first place).

If you have a large renovation in mind, break it up into a series of mini-projects. Complete one area before starting another (this is not always possible, say when working on a combined kitchen and family room). In any event, contain the work, and take a break before the next part of the renovation. Do not work without let-up until everything is completed—your family life will suffer.

Never start a messy, complicated or time-consuming task when there is not time to complete it. Starting demolition of a kitchen on Sunday night, knowing that you will not get back to it until the next weekend, is simply poor judgment. Not only do you not have use of the kitchen, you have a mess to live in. Add a vacation or personal day to a long weekend so that you have 3 or 4 days to do a complicated or time-consuming portion of the renovation. Save weeknights for hanging towel racks or putting up new mini-blinds.

Hire part-time help, college kids or day labor, to assist with heavy, messy projects. You get the mess out of the way, even though it costs a bit more. The savings in time will be huge.

The Resources

Home supply stores hold seminars and training for DIY types. Sign up—they are free. There are several excellent books on basic construction. Visit *www.amazon.com* and consider *The Complete Photo Guide for Home Improvement* (Creative Publishing International, 2005) or *Reader's Digest Book of Home Do-It-Yourself Projects* (Readers Digest, 1996).

21

Doing Part of the Work Yourself

The Challenge

Your goal is to keep costs down as much as possible. This is particularly true if you are a new homeowner or if your renovation plans are extensive and therefore expensive.

There are only a few ways to save: reduce the extent of the renovation, choose materials and finishes that are of lesser quality, reduce the costs of financing the project (lower interest rates) or get the labor costs under control.

You have decided to hire a contractor, as doing the work yourself is not an option. Naturally, you do not want to make substitutes on cabinets, flooring, fixtures or wall coverings. So the only other realistic option you have is reducing labor costs.

Your first challenge is to try to determine what the real labor costs are, based on the various contracts submitted by contractors. Typically, you would receive a total price for the work, the materials that you specified and a completion date. The contractor will not disclose hourly rates per labor category–e.g., skilled versus unskilled labor. Nor will the contractor disclose the mark-up on materials or subcontracted labor. Even if you try to understand the cost of the job based on a dollar average per square foot, you still cannot accurately determine labor costs. You can ask, but you would not get the information.

To reduce the total cost of the project, arrange to do some of the work yourself. But how much will you really save? Let us assume that you hope to do much of the unskilled work, demolition, clean-up, disposal and general site maintenance. These are the least expensive labor costs, perhaps involving day labor hired through a labor exchange. Further, you need a contractor willing to take the job at a smaller billed rate.

Your biggest challenge may be your ability to stick to your part of the bargain. It takes real dedication and motivation to demolish walls on Saturday and Sunday, or to rent a truck after work and take two loads to the city dump.

The Facts

Contractors want the biggest billable project for the time invested (bidding on projects, meeting with the architect and client, planning and managing the work). In terms of unbillable hours, it can cost the contractor as much to do a small job as a large one.

By doing some of the work yourself, you reduce the billable dollars for the project (that is, the overall value of the contract), which affects the contractor's ability to cover overhead, equipment and non-wage labor costs. Remember, you cannot determine how much of profit and overhead are buried in the non-skilled portion of the job. Demolition and disposal might seem complicated and more expensive than perhaps they really are. The contractor can therefore attach a greater dollar amount to these activities than they are really worth.

Contractors, as a rule, do not want to work as partners with homeowners—they do not have control over your time, your commitment and the quality of your work. If you agree to take over all demolition and disposal, to keep the work site clean and to do the grunt work getting supplies and materials, how does the contractor ensure that you actually do your part of the work? His or her goal is to do the best job at the least personal cost, to bill at or above the going rate, and to move on to another job. Down time is a real killer for contractors. If you have not secured materials for the plumbers on time, it means that two or three very expensive tradespeople might be sitting around drinking coffee.

Builders have every incentive to keep control of the purchasing function, as they often get discounts on materials (which are not passed on to you in the quote). In fact, there often is an additional mark-up on materials. If you now take over that function, it adversely affects the contractor.

In addition, by being an active participant in the construction work, you might end up diminishing the benefits of a signed contract. For example, you risk disputes that might otherwise have been clear-cut if the contractor controlled all aspects of the job.

Let us assume that you have found a contractor willing to work with you as a partner. Here are some of the activities non-skilled homeowners might take on without getting into too much trouble:

- Site preparation, such as removing shrubs and trees, sidewalks or tearing down an aging fence.
- Non-structural demolition, such as removing interior walls, cabinets and old flooring.
- Daily site clean-up.

- Rubbish removal, filling the dumpster, separating recyclable materials.
- Installing rolled insulation in walls.
- Priming, painting and papering walls.

The Solutions

If you are committed to doing some of the basic work yourself, get bids from contractors who are willing to partner with a homeowner. Advertise your request for bids on that basis. Do not wait until the contractor has bid on the job, and then try to negotiate a better deal with the offer of labor or materials procurement.

As a rule, larger renovation companies will not want to work with homeowners on a partnership basis. They have more to risk and greater overhead. No matter what size company you ask for bids, consider getting the preliminary work done *before* the bids are let. If, for example, you have already torn down the garage or completed the interior demolition of the basement, it is clear to everyone where your job ends and the contractor's begins.

If you are more skilled, engage a contactor to build the shell; you and your labor pool will complete the interior finishes. This is often done in new construction, particularly basements or bonus rooms above the garage. Buyers save substantial money at the time of purchase; the roughed-in plumbing and wiring are there for future development. Many contractors do not want to bid on painting; they probably do not keep full-time painters-on staff and it is a low-margin activity. They would prefer that this be handled by the homeowner, either as a DIY project or through a painting contractor.

No matter what approach you take in your efforts to reduce costs, learn the real costs of labor. If a skilled tradesman makes $25 an hour, the actual cost to the contractor is closer to $55 an hour when FICA, insurance, bonding, state unemployment, vacations and holidays and other labor costs are included. However, do not assume that these costs necessarily apply. Find out early who is and is not an actual employee of the firm. Full-time employees cost substantially more than sub-contractors or day labor.

If you chose to take on demolition—and disposal of the debris—learn something about the costs and limitations involved. Some dumpsters and disposal sites are limited to certain kinds of debris. Your contractor may have an existing contract for disposal or gets volume rates, whereas as a one-time customer, you get no discounts. Study the full costs of the project you take on to save money. There may be false economies in some of your assumptions.

Make sure not only that your homeowner's liability insurance is up to date, but also that it is increased during the time of construction. This is not very costly, but is very worthwhile. If you or someone from the construction crew gets hurt as a result of your negligence, you may have to cover the costs. Remember, you have agreed to do work, so you are now a partner, not just a customer.

Dumpsters are expensive. Be neat and orderly when filling them. You pay extra if the materials are not placed in the receptacle correctly, if you put in the wrong things or if you fill them over their limit. A dumpster of 25 cubic feet costs more and there are limits to where you can store it during construction. Know the local ordinance and make arrangements with your neighbors, especially if space is tight. Explain that you will do your best to get the dumpster out of sight as soon as possible, and that you will clean the area around the bin.

The Resources

Chapter 27: *Using the Big Box Building Center to Your Best Advantage* discusses what services and information home supply stores can provide. Use those services if you plan to participate in the renovation project, even in a minor way. Classes and general information abound if you look for them.

In addition, cable TV is filled with DIY shows, from landscaping to complete home makeovers. And why not ask friends and neighbors to work for you? Give them incentives to do so.

Health and Safety for the Do-It-Yourselfer

The Challenge

Chapter 22: *Health and Safety for the Do-It-Yourselfer* addressed general health
and safety issues. As your own general contractor or the primary worker on
site, there are specific concerns that need your attention. Remember—you bear
all the risk for health and safety problems. (If you hire subcontractors or have
installation from the large home supply stores, they should have the appropriate
insurance in case of accidents or damage.)

In the haste to get work completed or get the renovation site cleaned up, you
will be tempted to overlook important health and safety issues. The goal here
is to build on the information from the previous chapter and focus attention on
additional health and safety concerns *when you do not have the benefit of expert
advice from a full-time, active contractor.*

Health and safety issues are always more challenging when the home being
renovated is more than 30 years old. Past standards were very different from
today's. Most homeowners can recognize some of the larger housing issues
previously mentioned: mold, radon, lead paint and asbestos, etc. But there are
also other problems.

The Facts

Some housing still has *knob and tube* electrical wiring, which is typically
associated with a minimum electrical service of 60 amps. Any house that has had
even minimal work in the last 20 or 30 years would have had this wiring replaced
and the electrical service improved to at least 100 amps. However, older parts of
the house—perhaps an attic, garage or other out-building—still might have this kind
of wiring. It is unsafe, and must be replaced.

Of further concern is whether previous owners had replaced aluminum wiring
with the more conventional and safer copper wiring standard. Even copper

wiring could be a problem if it has a cloth/paper covering rather than the current standard of vinyl or plastic.

Many homeowners get a nasty surprise during renovation when they find that the house or adjacent property contains a tank used for storing heating oil. While underground storage tanks (USTs) must be disclosed when a property is sold, this is a fairly recent policy. If you have been in the house for 10 or 15 years, you might not be aware of a UST on your property.

USTs have to be dealt with. They corrode and leak, and are an environmental hazard. Even if the tank was professionally emptied years ago, it is nearly impossible to remove all the oil. As USTs age, they rust and deteriorate, contaminating the soil and ground water around it. Further, they can collapse, making the ground above unsafe. If the UST is stable, local laws may not require it to be removed. However, communities increasingly want USTs out of the housing stock and any environmental damage remedied.

Urea-formaldehyde presents another little-known health risk. The material was used as insulation in wall cavities and is also found in resins, pressed wood and kitchen cabinets. While banned for a while by the Consumer Product Safety Commission, there was insufficient evidence to eliminate it completely. It was suspected of causing cancer or, at the very least, eye and skin irritations. The good news is that this kind of insulation tends to release less and less formaldehyde over time. There are kits to determine if levels are high in your home.

Now on to some more basic, everyday health and safety issues for the DIY homeowner.

The Home Safety Council reports that 150,000 people went to the emergency room for injuries from using a ladder (and that is just *reported* accidents). See The Solutions at the end of this chapter for tips on ladder safety.

Be realistic about what you can and cannot do alone. Often, some help from a friend or spouse will make the work not only quicker, but safer. And when working, wear steel-toed work boots and protective headgear.

Electrical equipment and outlets must be properly used and maintained. Most major electrical work usually requires a separate permit. Many utilities will not connect a new service without an inspection and the proper permits. Such work, along with heating and air conditioning, is often best left to professionals.

Most injuries in the home result from falls. The State of Home Safety in America says that falls are by far the leading cause of death—nearly 6,000 each year.

In addition, 5.1 million injuries are reported. Homeowners are not nearly as conscious or concerned about fall as professionals, making basic planning and a tidy work site all the more important.

When you hire a contractor, you also take advantage of various services for the removal and disposal of construction debris. Doing it yourself requires some basic information about what can and cannot be done. A city or suburb may take a good deal of the debris from your construction site. It is better to stagger this over an extended period of time, rather than asking them to pick up a huge load. Further, your chances of the local service helping are improved if you are scrupulous about the items you are leaving for collection. Do not put out paints, thinner, asbestos, oil, grease–even dirt and brick.

Some cities will respond to a special collection, though you may be charged. If the city has hired a private contractor to collect garbage, you *will* be charged. If the renovation is large enough, you will need a dumpster. These not only come in different sizes, they also have limits on how high you can fill them and what you can put in them. Dirt, bricks, trees and shrubs may be collected but must be separated from wood, plaster, pipes, siding and other *normal* building materials. Disposal companies have strict regulations about what can and cannot go into a landfill. Toxic or hazardous material must go into specially constructed, lined disposal sites, which are expensive.

You may need a permit for a dumpster and there may be restrictions where it can be placed. Place the dumpster as close to the work site as possible. Try to get a dumpster you can open from the back. Lay the materials as flat at you can and fill in between with small debris. Break down old cabinets, small walls or stairs to their component parts. To minimize costs, try to organize your debris so that you do not order the dumpster until you absolutely have to. When done, move it as soon as you can.

You could use a truck or van to take small loads to the local dump. Again, there is a good chance of being charged per load, so make it worth your while. The same issues about toxins and forbidden materials apply here.

Many municipalities have extensive recycling sites and facilities. There are also not-for-profit groups that will accept household items in good condition. Perfectly good materials are often tossed because the new owner has a different concept for the house. This is an enormous waste. If you cannot recycle, try to donate.

The Solutions

Ladders are one of the homeowner's essential tools, and there are new and better kinds being marketed every day. Do not use a metal ladder. Wooden ladders are too heavy. The best choice is a more expensive composite ladder—you will not have to worry about coming in contact with power lines.

For every four feet the ladder extends up, you should move it one foot away from the base: the 4-1 rule. When your belt buckle reaches the top of the ladder, go no farther up. Use scaffolding with dual ladders if you are doing extensive work. Tie the ladder to the building while working and do not overreach.

These days, most paints and stains are not combustible, although cleaning fluids (turpentine and benzene) may be. When using these products, ventilate the room by opening the windows, clean spills immediately, store rags in a closed container and use a face mask and eye protection, especially if you are using any kind of pressurized paint. The best safety glasses are those that have side shields (especially important when using power tools).

Build temporary structures like rails and fences to protect you from falling from a height. Portable railings securely fastened ensure that you have something to back you up should you lose your balance. They also provide a grab bar in case of a fall.

The Resources

An extensive construction and safety manual is provided by Construction Safety Association of Ontario. You can download the entire 232-page manual for free at *www.csao.org*. The information sets a high standard, is worth reading and in many cases is worth implementing. Everything from first aid to working in confined spaces is discussed.

23

Should You
Live In or Move Out
During Construction?

The Challenge

Deciding whether or not to live in a house during construction can be very difficult. Your choice affects the quality of your life as well as your renovation budget. A large factor in this decision is how much of the work is being done at one time. Unless you can somehow isolate the rest of the house, a major renovation will probably require you to move until the work is completed.

Here are some issues to consider:

- Are you adding an addition which abuts or flows into living space?
- How much is being done at one time?
- Will all or part of the house be open to the elements?
- How many people (and pets) are involved?
- What are the ages and health of the family members?
- What is your general tolerance level?
- What are the trade-offs? One bath instead of two, for instance.
- Are there safe rooms–places that are clean, dry and comfortable?
- Can you relocate functions to another room?
- How comfortable are you having strangers in your home while living there?
- Do you have a home business?
- Can the construction crew maintain the integrity of the workspace versus the rest of the house?
- Can you seal off the construction area from the rest of the house?

There are issues you must consider if you decide to move out during construction:

- The cost. It can be very expensive to rent and renovate at the same time.
- Will a short-term move affect your children's schooling and social life?
- How do you communicate your decision to younger children?
- You are not going to live as comfortably in rental space as you did at home.
- Close quarters may increase the stress and tension.

- How much do you need to be on-site during construction to make decisions?
- It may not be easy to find short-term leases for adequate housing.
- What will you do to protect furnishings and household goods during construction?
- What about security after the workers have left and you are not on the premises?

The Facts

Temporary housing can be expensive. Check the local paper or consult a real estate agent about possible alternatives. If the lease is less than a year, or is month to month, you can expect to pay more than if you signed a lease for 1 year. If the housing is furnished, rates increase proportionately. Like any other renter, you will have to pay a security deposit and will be asked to fill out a rental application, which involves a credit check.

Is the cost of temporary housing in your budget? Be realistic from the beginning. If your renovation project involves several rooms, particularly areas like the kitchen and family room, it is hard to live and renovate in the same house. Frequently, families assume that they can tough it out, but end up moving to temporary housing.

The quality and location of temporary housing affect the costs greatly. If you intend to live close to your house during construction and if you live in a popular or expensive area, expect to pay a great deal more. Shop wisely, and try to achieve a balance between cost and convenience.

Many landlords do not allow pets. Others may limit the number of people in the rented accommodation. If you rent a house, what are your maintenance responsibilities? The lease you sign is a binding, legal document, so do not assume you can work around it. If it has been a while since you last rented, go over the lease carefully. Get your attorney to read it.

You have rights as a renter. If you are denied housing, that denial must be for legitimate business reasons–for example, a poor credit history or a short time in your job. (The fact that you own your home will usually enhance your standing with a landlord.) You cannot be denied housing because of your race or the fact that you have children (unless it is a restricted community).

Whether you move out or stay in, there is increased pressure to finish the work as quickly as possible. Do not allow quality to suffer. The pressure will increase exponentially if the project is delayed. Try to get everything in perspective. Weigh the need for quality renovation against the costs of alternative housing.

What health issues will arise if you live in the house? (Chapter 22 discusses health and safety in more detail.) Asthmas, allergies and respiratory problems are of particular concern: fine dust and particles can aggravate an existing condition. If either lead paint or asbestos is known to exist in the house, special measures must be implemented. These can be very costly.

Some parts of construction are worse than others: for example, demolition of walls and ceilings, and sanding taped dry wall. The dust, smell and mess can be extreme. Protecting your furniture, heirlooms and household goods can be complicated and expensive, especially if part of the home is open to the elements, even briefly. How much of your property can you safely store in the house without damage? Can you afford a storage service?

The Solutions

If you move during construction, look for a house that is for sale. The seller may be willing to rent for a while. Of course, you may get settled in, only to have the house sold beneath you. See if the local university has professors on sabbatical whose houses may be available for rental. Or you can sign up for a house-sitting service. In any case, ensure that any agreement is flexible, allowing for extensions should your renovation take longer than scheduled.

Whether you live in or move out, some or all of your furniture and household goods will need to be stored safely. The storage area could be your basement, garage or attic. Also, see if you can move some or all of the goods to a friend's or family's house to save money. Alternatively, you may want to put it in temporary storage. Storage companies have new systems where a unit is dropped at your house, you or your workers fill it and then it is whisked off site. As always, find out the costs before making any decision.

If you live in, discuss with your contractor ways to limit the inconvenience and mess. While plastic sheeting and duct tape never seal completely, they are a good start. You may put two plastic walls in place, one a foot or two away from the other, working on the assumption that plaster dust will get through one but not the other. Or you can build a false or temporary wall (with 2 x 4s and plywood) to limit exposure. This, too, needs to be sealed with plastic and tape. The small bit of damage that such a structure will cause can easily be repaired with joint compound and paint.

Try to ensure that the entrance to the workspace does not involve the livable portion of the house. This can be a real problem if you allow workers to use the phone or bathroom.

You or the contractor must take responsibility for cleaning in and around the worksite. Not only do larger pieces of debris need to be removed, but major surfaces–including the floor, stairs and other flat surfaces–must be swept and cleaned. Dust, nails, solvents, paints and tools should be removed, thrown away or stored accordingly.

Some portion of the renovation project is always the worst: consider timing this work while you are on vacation or on a family trip. You can maintain direct communication with your contractor by fax, phone and e-mail. Photos can be attached to e-mail so that you can keep current.

The Resources

There are several efficient Websites that assist in finding temporary housing. Visit *www.corporatehousing.com* to locate various options using the handy city and state locator. This site and others offer extended-stay hotels, corporate apartments, furnished condos–even vacation and private homes. Similar sites include *www.extendedstayhotels.com*, which offers hotel suite options in every part of the country. If you visit *www.rentnet.com*, you receive not only leads for rental apartments and corporate housing, but useful information about renting, moving pets and more.

One solution–space and zoning laws permitting–is to rent a recreational vehicle (some are quite spacious and, of course, expensive) and live on your property during construction. Visit the RV industry's national organization at *www.rvra.org* for rental information and to locate a dealer in your area.

24

Neighbors and Noise

The Challenge

If you happen to have the worst house on the block and decide to make it the best house on the block, your immediate neighbors will be your best friends and supporters, delighted that the old house will be rejuvenated.

However, if you do the work yourself, or stage the renovation over a long period of time, be warned—your neighbors might support you up to a point, but they will tire quickly when progress stalls or is slow.

No matter the condition of your home, if you have hired a contractor and the renovation project is of limited duration, your neighbors will be happier. All the same, it will be natural for them to have concerns about what is going on, whether it is to code, how much it will inconvenience them, and so forth.

If your suburb is an area where tear-downs are increasingly common, the novelty wears off very quickly. Neighbors who do not want the neighborhood to change or cannot improve their own homes to the same extent may become embittered about the noise, mess and inconvenience.

If homes are close together and easements are tight, there is almost always going to be sensitivity about construction debris, ladders, the look of the back (or front) yards and every space in-between. In some popular city neighborhoods, the street may be lined with workers' trucks, making parking (difficult at the best of times) impossible.

The Facts

An informal survey of homeowners found that the major sources of conflict with neighbors during renovation projects were:

- Workers parking on the street.
- Blocked driveways, garages and alleys.

- Double parking on the street.
- Messy work site.
- Work site that is not secured.
- Damage to fences, landscaping or the neighbor's house itself.
- Temporary interruption of gas, water or electrical service.
- Very loud construction noise.
- Prolonged construction noise.
- Delivery trucks that block the street while unloading.
- Open dump trucks hauling away debris or bringing gravel or sand–they often spill on the street and parkway.
- Work starting too early or continuing into the evening.
- Failure to pick up debris around the neighbor's house.
- Workers on site over the weekend.
- Toxic odors and smells.
- Garish designs or colors.
- Portable toilets.
- Renovation project perceived as too large for the site (even if it is within code).
- New construction that blocks views or sunlight.
- Temporary work lighting.
- Overflowing dumpsters.
- Contractors who do not speak English.
- Perceived danger to children and pets.

The situation can become very tense if the renovation is lengthy or complicated and if the neighbors are home all day. In fact, a new term has been coined to reflect this growing anger: *remodeling rage*.

Neighbors can also simply give in to feelings of envy as first one, then two, then more neighbors start remodeling their houses. In such situation, people react negatively because they wish that they were able to participate in the remodeling boom going on around them.

Many communities have not solved the McMansion battle that raged throughout the 1990s. *RealEstateJournal.com* reports that the average house size has increased by 10 percent in the last decade, while the average lot size decreased by 10 percent–setting the stage for bitter fights over how much house is right per square foot of lot. Even though some limits have been imposed by city councils and other governing bodies throughout the United States, many residents find the efforts to limit the size of new housing and additions ineffective and unsatisfactory. Individuals opposed to increasing house size say that building and zoning codes are badly outdated.

One approach used to limit renovations and increases in house sizes involves putting whole neighborhoods on special historical registers, which means that the buildings cannot be altered or torn down. Many people believe that this approach infringes basic property rights–particularly when the houses are of no significant architectural merit (and are protected simply because the city council wants to limit house size). Those who oppose such moves insist that limiting house size adversely affects the future value of their homes.

Neighbors living near construction are especially irritated when the homeowners are absent during construction. For the homeowners, moving to temporary housing during renovation may be sensible and necessary. However, it may rankle neighbors who cannot move during your construction and have no one to complain to when something unpleasant happens.

Many homeowner and condominium associations are not rehabber friendly. Their rules can severely limit what can be done and when. High-rise owners learn the hard way that construction materials and work are adversely affected by the availability (or unavailability) of elevators to get to the remodeling site. Whether a high-rise or a homeowners association, walk into the renovation project with your eyes wide open. Know the rules.

Some remodelers who specialize in high-rise work ask to inspect the adjoining properties–on both sides and below. A simple matter of wall-to-wall mirrors in the next unit changes the way work is done in your condo. Taking detailed pictures of common walls and floors may prevent complaints and lawsuits over real or perceived damages to adjoining units.

The Solutions

There is no easy or fool-proof way to satisfy all the neighbors' demands (reasonable or not) and still get your remodeling done in an efficient, timely and cost-sensitive way.

Rather than simply ignoring potential problem or insisting it is your right to do what you want with your property, reach out to neighbors. Visit each of them, even if you do not know them particularly well. Explain that you are renovating your house. Give them an estimated schedule for the work, but never commit to a firm date for completion.

Insist that your contractor also make an effort to communicate with the adjoining homeowners, or at least be available if someone has a complaint. Do not ignore any issue, no matter how trivial it seems–though do not go too far the other way, either, by conceding every single point.

There is nothing like common sense and simple courtesy. Take the time to find out what your neighbors are concerned about. Limit the workday so that your neighbors do not have to listen to the noise during dinner or evening hours. If you specify that work will end at a certain time of the day, makes sure it ends at that time. If the situation calls for it, compromise. For example, do not start demolition if the neighbors are having an anniversary or graduation party the next day. In addition, insist that your contractor follow some basic rules:

- Limit loud noise work to the middle of the day.
- Keep radio noise down.
- Make an effort to screen out some of the mess or equipment.
- Place the dumpster as far as possible away from the neighbors.
- Avoid using leaf blowers to remove dust.
- Keep the dumpster covered when not in use.
- Be sensitive about parking.
- Turn off equipment and vehicles when not in use.
- Place portable toilets in less visible locations, like the back of the property; make sure that the toilets are serviced regularly.
- Control dust with water and chutes.
- Take care of the neighbors' fences, trees and houses.

Do not go onto the neighbors' property for any reason without their consent; if you need access frequently, get permission in writing.

Invite the neighbors to your house for a brunch or yard party and make them feel like they are part of the process. Motivate even the grumpiest with the expectation that your work will increase the value of their homes also.

Move the project along as best you can, being sensitive that everyone gets tired of looking at a long, drawn out renovation. Even the best neighbors are going to get tired of the mess. A small gift or a simple apology is going to go a long way if matters really get difficult, and always remember that an apology is infinitely cheaper than a lawsuit.

The Resources

Two Internet sites offer a great deal of information about the law, neighbors and other issues that arise during construction. Visit *www.findlaw.com* or *http://forum.freeadvice.com* for free information.

25
Do-It-Yourself
Kitchen Remodeling

The Challenge

Could you take on the remodeling of your own kitchen (with the aid of some friends and a professional or two) and make it work? Well, if you are a little bit handy, it is perfectly possible. Before taking on any new project, however, see Chapter 20, *Should You Do the Renovation Yourself?*

There is only one kitchen in your house, so the longer it is out of service, the more difficult it is for everyone. Your challenge, therefore, is not only to do the work, but to do it in a timely fashion.

If you can allocate only weekends to renovating a kitchen on your own, the work could take months. Try putting together a block of time–say vacation plus weekends or a holiday–that allows you to work for several days in a row. Further, consider the extent of the remodeling. If, for instance, you are basically keeping the same footprint of cabinets, appliances and center island, the job will be much easier than if you are expanding or rearranging the kitchen.

Do you have a convenient place to set up a temporary kitchen during construction? A basement, sun porch or even the garage (in warm weather) might do. Remember, you need access to water and move the old refrigerator to the temporary location. Forget the stove, as you can always have a microwave, crock pot or electric oven for temporary cooking.

Finally, it is essential that everyone in the house buys into the do-it-yourself program. Nothing will make matters worse than if the household is not supportive and willing to assist.

The Facts

Do-it-yourself kitchen remodeling is complicated. Count on it taking 50 percent more time than you allocate. Further, if you work long hours, you will get tired, which will make quality work difficult. Save the mindless work–such as cleaning the work site or driving to the garbage dump–until day's end.

Preparation is the key to a successful job:

- In most areas, you need a permit to renovate a kitchen. Do not wait until the last minute.
- Make quality drawings or plans of the intended work. If you cannot do this, hire a designer to do them.
- Learn to use a CAD/CAM design software so you can get an idea of the result before you begin work.
- If you need a dumpster, get it before tearing out the old kitchen.
- List what is to be saved and where it will be stored.
- Write a basic inventory list: drywall, screws, sub flooring, studs, etc.

Some of the most common mistakes when doing it yourself are:

- Damaging the walls you plan to keep when removing old cabinets.
- Damaging counters, cabinets or floors you plan to reuse (or give away).
- Failing to turn off all the utilities before beginning work.
- Trying to get too much done too quickly.
- Not seeking help or advice (remember all the resources that home supply stores have).
- Getting dust and debris in adjoining rooms.
- Not having access to a dolly or hand truck to move heavy objects.
- Failing to organize the work site.
- Not planning the project to use time and materials well.

Door openings must be large enough for the new appliances and cabinets. Some key measurements are crucial if the work and traffic patterns in your kitchen are going to work well for everyone:

- Doorways at least 32 inches wide.
- Seating area 36 inches wide.
- Wall cabinets at least 12 inches deep and 30 inches high.
- Base cabinets at least 21 inches deep.
- Clearance space of 30 inches between a stovetop and unprotected surfaces above.
- Counter heights 36 to 45 inches above the floor.
- Landing space of at least 15 square inches next to a stove or microwave.
- Counter corners be rounded or softened.
- Doors and drawers that do not bump into each other.

Cabinet installation can be tricky. Some typical mistakes are:

- Hanging the upper cabinets incorrectly.
- Not attaching cabinets to the studs.
- Damaging the cabinets.

- Not aligning the cabinet doors.
- Damaging newly built or repaired walls during installation.
- Not cutting the sink opening to the right size.
- Fitting and installing drop-in appliances improperly.

Finally, get out your checkbook. Estimates from *www.Fineliving.com* show that a low-end renovation project can range from $5,000 to $12,000; the middle range goes up to $48,000; and the higher end is $50,000 or more!

The Solutions

Before you start, box up everything that will not be used in your temporary kitchen. Label the boxes and store them out of the way. Remove anything that is not nailed or screwed down. If something needs to stay in the room, cover it with plastic and tape the plastic to seal it.

Seal the room from the rest of the house. That means having access to a bathroom without tripping through the rest of the house. Put up at least two plastic, wall-to-wall and floor-to-ceiling barriers. Use lots of tape and do not worry about damaging the walls—a little joint compound and paint will solve any problems.

During demolition, curb your enthusiasm and that of your co-workers. Make sure that you are taking out only walls that you do not want. You may want to keep the framing, but just need to replace only the plaster/drywall.

Removing appliances, including disconnecting the utilities, requires care. Consult the instructions for the individual appliances. If you no longer have the literature or something is not clear to you, seek professional advice, especially if you plan to keep the appliances.

Turn off electric circuits to the area in which you will be working. Older homes could have multiple circuits in the kitchen. The wiring could have been changed and you may not be certain which circuits control which parts of the kitchen. Test all lights and outlets to make sure that they are off. Tape over the breakers so no one will turn them on by mistake. If you plan to upgrade your electrical system by adding new outlets and fixtures, dismantle all existing outlets and fixtures.

After removing all the light bulbs, dismantle each fixture by unscrewing the plate and receptacle, and pulling it out of the box. Put wire nuts on any exposed wires. The bare copper wire is the ground and does not need to be capped.

The more you can take furniture apart, the easier the demolition. Removing drawers, cabinet doors and shelves will reduce the weight of the cabinets and make it easier to remove them from the room. Take the back door off its frame and remove the screen door for the duration of the project. This will ensure that you get large objects out of the room without damage. By and large, you should take apart the kitchen in reverse order of installation (see below).

There is, thankfully, a time when you begin to put it all back together. The first step, of course, is replacing or repairing the walls. Salvaging existing walls is worthwhile, assuming that it does not take more time to patch them than to replace them. If the damage is limited to cracks and small holes, consider repairing it. Remember that you can repair larger portions by backing the holes with drywall and filling the missing surface with joint compound or plaster.

According to www.*DoItYourself.com*, this is the order in which you should build your new kitchen:

- Rough in framing and walls
- Finish walls
- Prime and paint
- Ceramic tile, vinyl or hardwood flooring*
- Wall cabinets
- Base cabinets and islands
- Cabinet doors, drawers and hardware
- Plywood base for tile countertops
- Recessed sink
- Countertops–wood, marble, tile
- Surface mounted sink and fittings
- Disposal
- Dishwasher
- Ice-maker connection
- Over-the-range hood/vent
- Stovetop
- Wall oven and microwave
- Vinyl flooring*
- Range
- Refrigerator, freezer, trash compactor and icemaker
- Lighting fixtures
- Finishing touches–trim
   * Hardwood flooring and ceramic tile are always laid before cabinets are installed. Vinyl flooring can be placed after the cabinetry is in place.

The Resources

Visit *www.kitchens.com* for a style quiz to figure out whether you like contemporary or traditional or any style in between. The higher your score, the more you value a traditional look. The book, *Kitchens That Work: The Practical Guide to Creating a Great Kitchen* (Tauton, 1999), is a useful guide when planning your new kitchen. Visit *www.amazon.com* for additional information and other similar books.

26

New Materials for a New Age

The Challenge

Who would ever think of steel roofs, concrete kitchen counters or plastic cove molding and trim in the family room? Well, these and similar products and applications are here–and here to stay. Housing construction and renovation have come a long way, not only in terms of design and construction techniques, but also in the choices of material and how they are applied.

There are a variety of reasons for choosing materials that are atypical. Among them are:

- You want your renovation to be green (eco-friendly).
- You want to save money, as some newer materials cost less than traditional ones.
- You want to protect your home as well as possible against fire, earthquakes or hurricanes.
- You like the style or look of the new products.
- Your insurance company or local utility offers incentives to remodel differently with newer, safer products.
- You want to ensure that your renovations will last and require less maintenance.
- You are concerned about interior air quality and the use of some polyresins in your living space.

Whatever the motivation, be knowledgeable about the available choices. If you seek out alternatives, know that it will take longer to prepare for the renovation. Further, you may find it difficult to find a contractor who is familiar with new techniques and materials.

Also, you may be challenged from a variety of sources: a homeowners or historical committee that will seek to limit your material choices; building codes that may be out of date; the cost and availability of alternative materials; and less competitive bidding when the time comes to do the work. Do not be put off by the challenge, however. It is becoming increasingly easy to find not only the materials, but also the qualified contractors who can install and work with them.

The Facts

Several years ago, a homeowner in the earthquake-prone San Francisco area made the national news because he was building a concrete house. At first blush, it seemed ridiculous and rather out of place. Undeterred, he continued the project, finishing the house with natural stucco and a beautiful faux tile roof. Once completed, no one knew the difference. He received a huge reduction in homeowner's insurance and an energy credit from the local utility, as the mass of the structure substantially reduces both heating and cooling costs. This homeowner understood that there were alternatives to traditional stick building, and that while the initial cost may have been more, he would save money over time.

In some places in the West where fire is a common and a persistent threat during the dry season, homeowners are being forced to change roofing materials from traditional cedar to non-flammable materials like steel or tile.

A new trend in deck-building is to use a series of aluminum joists in combination with composite decking materials made from recycled wood products and resins. The beauty of this system is that the aluminum will last almost forever without painting or other maintenance. Color can be baked onto the structure to match the composite decking—almost any color you choose.

Many of the newer materials and installations come from industrial or commercial applications. For example, in lofts or other large spaces, glass blocks are frequently used instead of traditional sheet rock and stud walls. Typically, the primary natural light source in a loft is limited to one or two windows. Glass blocks provide a different look while allowing in more light.

Most downtown and commercial office space use aluminum studs instead of wood for interior walls. Generally the rationale is based on safety: in case of fire, there is less combustible material. But there are other reasons as well: the studs are a fixed height, are lightweight, are made of a renewable resource and provide an increasingly compelling alternative to common 2 x 4s. Many residential builders are following suit, and are using aluminum instead of wood.

Stainless steel is very popular as a clean, durable and stylish surface for appliances in the kitchen. It is now also becoming popular as a material for backsplashes and even counter tops. While for some people it may have an industrial look, stainless steel introduced into the home is both practical and appealing to those seeking alternatives to stone, wood and other hard surfaces.

You may not consider building your addition out of concrete, but you may choose to use it in a variety of applications in your home remodeling. Lite concrete is being used with greater frequency for roofing. Concrete can be formed to look like just about any roofing tile or surface—from styles like cedar shakes to traditional tiles to slate. Of course, the colors can match any existing roof or complement any exterior house décor.

Stamped and stained concrete has a variety of applications both inside and outside. Kitchen and bath floors and countertops are being made from designer concrete patterns. Shined, buffed and sealed, the hard surfaces can look as good as any other material, and last forever. Stamped concrete is increasingly being used outside for patios, driveways and other applications.

Some additional flooring alternatives are both old and new. Bamboo, a very renewable resource—depending on the kind you choose—is an extremely fashionable, durable and eco-friendly material that is finding its way into more and more renovations. Additionally, consumers are looking for new woods from Brazil (jatoba, or Brazilian cherry), Bolivia (Patagonian teak and white tigerwood), as well as recycled hardwoods originally used in industrial and commercial properties.

What is old is now new. Linoleum, synonymous with flooring in the 1940s and 1950s, is an example. It is new in that it looks like other floor applications such as hardwood; it is old in that it is exactly the same product that was sold years ago—a combination of resin, linseed oil, wood byproducts and cork. Its renewed popularity stems from the fact that it is eco-friendly, durable (lasting up to 40 years) and biodegradable.

A very interesting and attractive alternative for flooring and walls is leather tiling. Made from the same material used in shoe soles, it is a highly pleasing surface that is soft underfoot, sound-absorbing, fire-retardant and easy to maintain with soap and water. Strange as it may seem, leather is also highly durable, ideal for bedrooms, family rooms, libraries and home theatres, though it is not recommended for potentially humid or wet locations, such as baths and kitchens.

Cork flooring is rather new in North America, but has been common in Europe for the last 100 years. Cork is renewable, so it is environmentally friendly. It is soft under foot, is sound-absorbent and once it is sealed, can be used almost anywhere. In fact, one of the best uses of cork is the kitchen. It can be repaired easily and withstands lots of traffic.

Finally, think of glass as an innovative and useful remodeling alternative. Glass is used in tiles, block, avant-garde room dividers and a host of other applications. It is stronger than it looks, easy to clean, bright, modern and stylish.

The Solutions

Because you have so many alternatives in new products and materials and their applications, it is difficult to evaluate what is best for your situation. Clearly, if you are entertaining some of the alternative products discussed, and you are unfamiliar with them, you need education and information. Like every other aspect of home renovation, it is risky to go ahead without knowing what you are in for, the costs and whether you can find the materials and installers you need.

The best advice is to see these materials already in use in a home setting, and to spend some time talking to people who have chosen them. Every home renovation product has advantages and disadvantages, so before you march off and spend a good deal of money, make sure you know about applications, cost and maintenance.

The Resources

While there are dozens of Websites on all the various products and materials discussed above, visit *www.builddirect.com* for a good sampling of products used for flooring, roofing, siding, decking and countertops. This site will provide a start as you begin to explore the alternatives.

Visit *www.ecotimber.com* to find a variety of environmentally friendly flooring choices. Each material presented is rated in terms of its ecological and environmental friendliness.

27

Using the Big Box Building Center to Your Best Advantage

The Challenge

To be on top of your remodeling project, you need all the resources and high-quality information you can get. As pointed out many times in this book, planning (contracts, money, materials and more) is of the uppermost importance. In order to bring your plan to fruition, you need to get down and dirty. Clipping articles from the paper, taking pictures of other people's renovations and improvements, and building up a stack of the popular home and garden magazines are an excellent start. But you need to see, feel, touch and examine the goods that will go into your project.

Start by learning about commodity items such as pipe, sheet rock and plywood. They might not seem of interest to you, but that makes it all the more important to find out what they are and when they are used. Then take a trip to the contractor's side of the building supply store. If you are putting in a chair rail, crown molding or other decorative details (at significant additional cost, based on whether you use common pine or hardwood oak), then a visit to the *other side* is even more important. Get a sense of the prices on all commodity materials, as well as other decorative supplies.

You would not buy a car without kicking the tires. The same is true for the big-ticket items that are part of your renovations. Your challenge is to try to understand and evaluate the relationship between the quality and pricing of these major items: appliances, bathroom fixtures, cabinets, carpeting and more. (Cabinets are particularly vexing, as you need to compare not only style, but materials, size and hardware.) The combinations are almost infinite: stock items versus semi-custom versus custom.

The Facts

Commodity items like lumber are priced by the piece (2 x 4 lumber, sheets of plywood). Other basic building supplies are priced by the linear foot (specialty items like base board molding) or by the square foot/yard (carpeting, for example). Some items, like man-made counter tops or marble are not only priced by quality and square foot, but also by thickness.

If you are inexperienced in renovation, you would be amazed at how many pieces of lumber go into building one interior wall (non-load bearing). Start to multiply the bits and pieces of construction, and you will see why it is so expensive.

As a rule, materials will represent anywhere from 40 percent to 50 percent of your renovation budget. You can substantially reduce (or add) to the cost of the project by your choices of finished materials (as opposed to the commodity items). Finished materials represent what is actually on display: cabinets, flooring, wall covering and countertops. There will be trade-offs: for example, you probably should go for cheaper carpeting if you have three dogs and kids and the flooring is going to be replaced in 5 years anyway.

Home improvement stores have design centers that can prepare general specifications for your project. They can be particularly useful in helping you get your first, concrete plan on paper (whether it changes over time is not really important). The cost, if any, is minimal. You can see how the space works, what the traffic patterns might be, how the space might look next to existing rooms, and more.

The Solutions

Multiple visits to home improvements centers (big box stores) and specialty locations (e.g., for lighting and flooring) make the project real and concrete (no pun intended). Assuming that your first trip is to a large, general retailer, let us consider some of the advantages:

- A full range of products in all home-improvement categories (but a limited range within a specific grouping–kitchen appliances, say).
- General design assistance.
- A wide range of prices, but generally cheaper than boutique stores.
- Experienced, but average store personnel.
- In-store credit (although not any cheaper than credit cards).
- Seminars and in-store training if you do the work yourself.
- List of contractors (may not be as reliable as other sources).
- Can do the work for you–for example, installing a new siding.

A large home center could potentially be your sub-contractor for many of your remodeling needs. This assumes that you are willing to take on the role of general contractor. The list of specialty tasks involved is almost endless: countertops, flooring, doors and windows, roofing, heating and air-conditioning, garage doors and openers, cabinets (including resurfacing), siding, decks, fencing, landscaping and more. As a rule, a home center will not act as a full-service contractor. (We have more to say about being your own general contractor in Chapter 19).

Some of the sub-contractors working with a home improvement center are not store employees, but are hired on a job-for-job basis. While their primary business is selling materials and supplies, services are a strategic necessity. When you get a quote for services, you should ask if the job is being completed by a company employee (or team of employees) or work-for-hire sub-contractors. Large retailers have a lot to lose if you are unhappy with work, especially if the workers are theirs. Either way, it will take time and effort to resolve any problems. Further, their services and materials should be evaluated just like any other builder or remodeler. As always: buyer beware.

You may have already determined that a specialty bath and shower establishment in a high-priced strip mall is out of your range. That does not mean that you should not visit the store. Talk with the help and learn why consumers would pay a premium for their goods. As a going concern, they compete with much larger, general retailers. There are reasons:

- The goods are superior, both in style and function.
- Stores employ above-average personnel to assist with design and questions.
- They offer personalized service, specifically a willingness to spend time with you.
- They can anticipate problems before they happen.
- They often have a short list of trusted contractors.
- They have access to a much wider range of products.
- They sell more specialty items (smaller sinks, larger ovens) than other outlets.
- They have an extensive cataloging system for more and varied manufacturers.
- They are very sensitive to word-of-mouth referrals and tend to solve disputes and problems quickly.
- They often offer free delivery as part of the order.

There are, of course, reasons not to use a specialty store:

- They sell at premium prices.
- There are times when average or above-average (at much lower prices) can look just as good and function equally well.
- Most items are special order; it takes weeks, even months, to get your items. This may play havoc with your schedule.
- There can be a restocking fee if an item is returned.

Wherever you visit, use a simple spreadsheet or chart like the one below to evaluate your choices. This example is for kitchen cabinets.

Product Comparison–Cabinets						Date:		
	Retailer	Manufacturer	Grade	Style	Hardware	Costs	Delivery cost	Available
Light Oak								
	Sears	Achme	stock	traditional	yes	$6,600	10%	7 days
	Home Depot	Smith & Co.	stock	traditional	yes	$6,200	10%	5 days
	Lowes	Smith & Co.	semi-custom	art/crafts	extra	$8,100	11%	10 days
	Specialty	Real Wood	custom	traditional	extra	$11,000	none	90 days
Cherry								
	Sears	Jones	semi-custom	art/crafts	yes	$7,900	10%	14 days
	Home Depot	Achme	semi-custom	art/crafts	yes	$7,500	10%	21 days
	Lowes	Jones	semi-custom	traditional	yes	$8,800	11%	14 days
	Specialty	Real Wood	custom	contemporary	extra	$12,300	none	120 days
Birch								
	Sears	Smith & Co.	stock	art/crafts	yes	$5,600	10%	7 days
	Home Depot	Smith & Co.	stock	traditional	yes	$5,700	10%	7 days
	Lowes	Achme	stock	contemporary	yes	$5,800	11%	7 days
	Specialty	Real Wood	custom	traditional	extra	$9,900	none	90 days

This chart can be download by going to www.encouragementpress.com

The Resources

Home Depot, Menards and Lowes all have extensive Websites and directories to find the nearest store. Visit *www.homedepot.com*, *www.menards.com*, or *www.lowes.com* for more information.

Some consumers prefer to work with local stores, often not as large. Many are neighborhood centers or hardware stores (some hardware stores have substantial home-improvement inventories). Visit *www.doitbest.com* and use the zip code locator to find a store near you.

Additional sites—and thus actual stores—to visit include *www.builderssquare.com*, *www.lowes.com* and *www.truevalue.com*. The latter has a wonderful resource called the Project Library, which offers all sorts of hints and information about home decorating and remodeling.

28

Buying the Best:
Custom Materials or
Will Off-the-Shelf Do?

The Challenge

What quality of materials is right for your renovation? This is difficult to answer without the specifics–particularly the extent of the renovation and the amount budgeted. And then you have to ask what is reasonable for the size of your house and neighborhood. You do not want to invest every spare dollar in a non-liquid asset (one that may not be convertible to cash in 6 months, say), but you also do not want to own an asset that you cannot sell for profit.

You now have to weigh what you *want* to do against what you *should* do. When considering what to include on your renovation list, focus on renovations that will sell. Try not to make your update too personal, too unconventional, too complicated. There is a tendency, especially if you have owned other houses, to make this one *special*–a word that is particularly difficult to define.

One family painted its Queen Ann stucco house a deep shade of purple–not everyone's taste by any means. But the rest of the house is quite traditional with hardwood floors and cherry kitchen cabinets. In this case, the special nature of the house can easily be changed with a new coat of paint.

Not so easy to correct is the very costly wine cellar where the formal dining room once stood or the 1,500 square foot workshop that replaced the three-car garage. Few future buyers will want to pay for your obsession. The more permanent (meaning structural) the changes, the more difficult it may be to sell them and the house, and you will end up wondering if you spent your scarce renovations dollars wisely.

The other side of the coin is to figure out what *should* be in a home of your size, price range and neighborhood. Certainly, your priority is to ensure your comfort and enjoyment, not to get what your neighbors have and you do not. However, if you live in a $600,000 neighborhood and you do not have central air conditioning or a second (or third) bathroom, perhaps your renovation plan is flawed. Again, trade-offs—what do you need, what do you want and what will sell? And do not assume that you will be in a house for a specified amount of time. Jobs come and go, and so do houses.

The Facts

Your primary challenge is to stay within your predetermined cost of renovation. If something is not in the budget, shelve it for the future. There are some features in a renovation that you cannot cut corners on: if the architect specified 2 x 6s used in exterior wall construction, you cannot arbitrarily cut costs by using 2 x 4s. There are many such examples. Further, local building codes define many of these specifications, so if you or the contractor make substitutions, you may not pass inspection.

Much of the cost of renovation is never seen. If the work is not accessible, you want to buy the best. Bathroom fixtures can easily be upgraded later. However, using sub-standard or minimal pipe, electrical wiring, heating and air conditioning ducts or insulation is just not worth it. If you have to tear down walls or rip up the floors in the future, you have saved nothing.

Buy the best heating and air conditioning you can afford. When in doubt, make the electrical service larger than you need; 200 amp service is not that much more expensive that 100 amp or 150 amp service.

Cheap (meaning substandard) windows and doors are a bad idea. On the other hand, you can save money by deciding to buy simpler windows, without built-in shades or fancy designs and shapes, features that do not affect the functionality of the windows.

As a rule, custom-ordered materials will cost more than semi-custom materials (which are not in stock at the store, but can be ordered from the specialty catalog). Both will cost more than what is in stock at the store. This is not an appeal for expediency or second-tier goods for your home; but it is a reminder that projects often get out of hand. You want to enjoy your home eventually, not be in perpetual construction.

Part of the trade-off in terms of materials and finishes may be the availability of the goods. Why put the family room renovation on hold while you wait 2 months for New England field stone, when an elegant local stone might do? Unless your architect, your builder and you are in complete coordination, special-order products can delay completion by weeks or months. Certainly, these features should be included if they are in the budget, if the neighborhood can bear the costs and if the time to get the materials is planned carefully.

When considering the details and the look of your renovation, there are some *great pretenders* available:

- Instead of cedar shakes for siding or roofs, use imitation ones made of recycled products. They will last longer (though be careful about the costs).
- Fiber-cement siding looks exactly like cedar siding, but is man-made and costs less. You can paint it to match existing wood siding.
- Stone veneer now looks the same around a fireplace as real stone. It is half the price and a fraction of the weight, which saves the cost of building a foundation or support in the basement.
- Laminate flooring is ideal for renovations projects such as basements, new space in the attic or a family room. It is durable, costs about one-half of hard wood and has a long warranty.
- Brick veneer is being increasingly used both inside and outside new construction and for renovation projects. It is lighter in weight and one-half the cost of whole brick.
- Stained cement is increasingly being used for kitchen floors and countertops. It is a whole new look, durable and cheaper than slate or marble.
- Polymer fencing looks like wrought iron. It is a bit cheaper than aluminum and about 30 percent cheaper than the real thing.
- Interior and exterior trim pieces made from a variety of man-made materials look like the real McCoy when they are painted. They are very durable and cost 75 percent less than traditional wood.

Most of these products are readily sold either online or at large retail stores. By considering all these, and more, you still might be able to afford the Sub-Zero freezer you always wanted!

One caution about man-made materials: some people have extreme allergies to manufactured materials like the ones listed above—even to certain types of carpeting. Exercise great caution if a family member is highly sensitive.

The Solutions

Start with the must-haves and work from there. You have done the budget and know the extent of the renovation, so go back and review the motivation for doing this work in the first place. You need a bigger kitchen, not necessarily a better one. Or you need a better one, not necessarily a bigger one. They are not the same.

Specify a combination of custom, semi-custom and off-the-shelf materials and fixtures. For example, you might choose above-average kitchen cabinets, but off-the-shelf light fixtures, or crown molding that is composite and painted, not oak and stained.

Should the best quality not be in line with your budget and/or schedule, prepare a savings list that specifies alternative choices. Use a spreadsheet to evaluate and cost the alternatives.

If your renovation includes the kitchen, ask yourself just how much you want to invest in appliances. A stove may be very important, but the refrigerator is not. Perhaps you do not care about the fancy bells and whistles on the dishwasher, but want the best for the laundry room. Buy the same style, not necessarily the same line, of appliances, and maybe not even the same level of quality within the same brand. This is sensible renovation.

The Resources

Reuse centers are the thrift stores of the home improvement industry. They take donated, used and surplus materials and sell them for substantially less than the retail price. You may save up to 80 percent of the manufacturer's suggest retail price (MSRP). Visit Websites such as *www.restoreonline.org* or *www.seconduse.com*, whose main mission is to keep building materials out of landfills. Habitat for Humanity has a nationwide chain of stores, the profits from which help fund their building programs. Visit *www.habitat.org* for more information.

Finally, companies such as Lumber Liquidators, a not for profit chain, offer big discounts on flooring and other products. Visit *www.lumberliquidators.com* and see how the prices stack up.

Green Is Good

The Challenge

Many homeowners are strongly conscious of environmental issues and are concerned about the kinds of products that they use their renovation. They wonder what impact their choice of products, materials and systems will have on air quality, the ozone layer and non-renewable resources. That is, they want their house to be as *green* as possible.

There are hundreds of ways to be green, some major, many minor. Nor do homeowners have to go green all the way. Partial substitutions are a good start, and some recycling is a small way to help the environment. Every step in this direction, homeowners and architects believe, will have an impact over time. Awareness of the green movement is growing, but there is a long way to go before green materials and practice become commonplace.

One of the challenges is to find design and construction specialists who are familiar with green materials and systems. While some products are already available at home building stores (man-made decking and siding materials, for example), going green in a major way is not necessarily simple or convenient. You need a different planning approach, one that requires a longer work schedule, somewhat specialized contractors and architects, and a thoughtful approach to your renovation—one based on an entirely different model.

It is extremely difficult to do comparisons of *normal* versus *green* renovation. Anecdotal evidence suggests that the initial costs may be as much as 10 percent higher for smaller green innovation to as much as 25 percent higher for a substantial green remodeling. The financial argument for going green is based not on short-term costs but longer-term savings. This argument may have merit, but it is not easy to demonstrate and will not come true unless you remain in your home for many years.

Take the example of replacing your home's furnace with a new, energy efficient model. Assuming that energy prices are relatively stable (which at this writing is not true), it might take 10 years to recover the initial investment. Dramatically increasing energy costs, however, may reduce that cost recovery model to 5 or 6 years. Assuming the normal 20- or 25-year life span of this furnace, the green replacement would therefore make financial (and environmental) sense.

In the end, being green comes down to environmental and financial issues; some homeowners may be willing to take risks on the latter in order to advance the former. Many feel that these are the trade-offs all homeowners ought to be willing to consider.

The Facts

The National Association of Home Builders has adopted a new Green Building Initiative, including voluntary guidelines for contractors and builders for new housing. Similar standards are being promulgated throughout the building trade industry. Going green is now a status symbol, with builders and developers routinely advertising that their housing meets the federal government's Energy Star energy-efficiency ratings.

If builders of new housing can be brought around to view green practices as good business and good marketing, such practices may be–and, truth be told, are being–carried over into the remodeling and renovation industry. Increasingly, homeowners have a greater choice of designers and contractors to assist them in their quest for green renovation.

The best way to understand the green movement is to offer examples of alternative products and systems. Energy efficiency is a major issue:

- Solar panels (photovoltaic systems) for electricity production.
- Passive solar heat (sun's rays on hard surfaces that hold the heat).
- Daylighting, controlling light (more in the winter, less in the summer).
- House fans to move cool air through a home.
- Incandescent lights replaced by compact fluorescent lamps.
- Trees and landscaping that reduces the need for air conditioning.
- Reversible duct systems that take the warm air from the top of the room to the living spaces below.
- In stick-built construction or renovation, a six-inch cavity for greater insulation.
- Thick concrete and foam wall systems that hold in heat and cooling.
- Eco-roofs–green planting on roofs.
- Heat pumps that take consistent temperatures from underground to replace or supplement HVAC systems.

- Programmable thermostats.
- Zone heating and air conditioning.
- Shading the outdoor air conditioning compressor.
- Thermal pane windows and insulated doors.
- New, efficient appliances and water heaters.

Green also includes the use of recycled or donated materials. For example:

- Donating cabinets, light fixtures, counter tops and flooring to recycling centers.
- Reclaiming lumber from either your home or buying existing lumber from the recycling center.
- Reusing brick, block or stone (the chunks of the old driveway, stacked rough side up can make a very nice retaining wall in the garden).
- Using recycled wallboard and insulation.
- Refinishing floors, trim or cabinets rather than replacing them.

In addition, there are some general guidelines that can contribute to a comfortable and beautiful green renovation:

- How and where you site your renovation—for example, by keeping mature trees and landscaping intact.
- Using rain barrels or other water storage systems to retain the water that comes from the roof and other hard surfaces.
- Preserving and protecting the topsoil during renovation.
- Planting evergreen trees on the north and northwest sides of the house to act as a natural windbreak during the winter.
- Paving driveways out of small stones, crushed oyster shells or other locally available materials.
- Less grass and more natural plantings that are native to your areas.
- Heavy use of mulch in the landscape to preserve water.
- Drip irrigations systems rather than broadcast sprinkler systems.
- Man-made materials for outside decks.

The Solutions

Going green takes considerable time and effort, especially in the planning stage. For example, it may take a while to locate some of the materials you need. Try to be flexible. Let us say you are looking for old-growth oak trim at a specified dimension; perhaps you should settle for smaller trim in oak or find an equally good substitute at the salvage yard.

You will need to work with a contractor who understands what you are trying to accomplish. Often the green rehabber can be an excellent source of products and materials, and can offer good advice. It is absolutely essential that you communicate to the builder your commitment to staying within your budget—just because you back green causes does not mean you have unlimited greenbacks.

Your choice of finishes is, of course, very important in your efforts to make your remodeling green-friendly. Choose trim and flooring materials that are from sustainable harvest wood, such as bamboo, which makes beautiful interior surfaces. Some of the new laminated flooring (a thin slice of veneer is backed by recycled composite board) means that you use less wood and still have the look and feel of traditional hard wood flooring. (By using these materials, you will also enjoy some substantial immediate savings.)

If you use brick, concrete, tile or fiber cement siding, not only are you green-conscious, but your work will last longer and require substantially less maintenance. Choosing laminated veneer lumber (LVL) for trusses and roofs means that you have purchased quality and strength, and have used a product from recycled wood scrap or fast-growing trees.

The not-so-big remodeling approach goes against the grain of current trends in housing, but staying within the original footprint of your house can represent a strong green statement. Try to anticipate how you or others might use your new space, and make the renovation as adaptable as possible without having to remove or add walls some time in the future.

Plan and create flexible usage space. For example, have the recreation room, home office and library part of the same room, rather than three specialized rooms. Consider redesigning unused or underutilized space. The big, old-fashioned dining room could become the new study and media center. You can still have a living room, but reduce its size in proportion to its use.

Finally, if you plan to recycle or salvage, the key is careful removal of materials; you need to protect them before they are sold, donated or salvaged. Used lumber for structural application should be used for interior work only. Old appliances should not be reused, as they are not energy-efficient.

The Resources

Much more can be found on this subject in books like *Green Remodeling: Changing the World One Room at a Time*, (New Society Publishers, 2004); visit *www.barnesandnoble.com* for details.

Visit *www.greensage.com* for an excellent online resource, including products, information, contractors and books. In short, everything you need for green renovation. They even have a wedding registry!

Windows and Lighting

The Challenge

One of the strongest trends in new home construction is opening the house to admit more natural light and arrange artificial light to eliminate shadowy spots. Nothing has more appeal than walking into a room with large windows; the effect is an open, comfortable and bright space.

Then there is the reality of increasing energy costs. Consumers in colder climates have seen tremendous price increases in natural gas and heating oil, to the point where electrical heat is now comparable in cost. In times of high energy prices, an expansive, open look may seem illogical. No matter how good the windows, you say, you are going to lose warmth or increase heat in your newly renovated house.

Further, the more glass you introduce, the more you need to be concerned about the cost of renovation and the care that must be taken when removing walls. New systems have to be put in place to support upper-stories and the roof. You just cannot cut holes and expect the integrity of the house to remain intact!

Thanks to new materials, including steel and laminated wood, the remodeling industry has changed the look of older houses. By allowing longer spans without upright supports, an open look can be achieved without concerns for the integrity of the home.

There are additional challenges: many older homes were designed with small windows, perhaps only one to a room. These days, interior walls are much less prominent, allowing one space to flow into another and natural light to flow from the south and east of a house to the northwest. Many contemporary high-rises were built on this principle: a wall of windows at one end that allows light to reach the interior of the apartment or condo.

Your challenge is to introduce more, functional light into the home without raising the costs beyond the point of negative return at resale time. Your goal is to create a friendly, warm and inviting space flushed with light, making the house attractive at resale.

Windows and lighting should be top priorities in your renovations plans.

The Facts

During a recent HGTV episode, the designers made one change in the living room that added, in their estimate, $10,000 to the house's value. The living room faced the north and northwest, and even with two windows was dark and shadowy. The house was a one-story, frame home, so adding a third window was easy and inexpensive. The after-effect was dramatic—a much brighter, more inviting room. The moral: everyone responds to natural light and an open look.

Window manufacturers are constantly improving their craft and products. The choices, sizes, materials and quality of new or replacement windows are excellent. Buy the best windows you can afford; best does not mean elaborate, but workable, cleanable, energy-efficient and, most importantly, large.

As important as windows are, it is the installation that makes them work. Two inexpensive items are the homeowners' friends: insulation and caulk. The cavity above and around the window needs to be completely insulated (hopefully, you can open the rest of the wall, and fill it as well). The area around the windows, both inside and outside, needs to be carefully caulked with quality, mildew-resistant, paintable and durable material. A few extra dollars on caulk will save maintenance and heating for years to come.

Large windows help integrate the garden, yard, deck or patio with the rest of the house—especially true during warmer weather, when the house tends to be open. A wall of windows, or its equivalent, may cause you to reconsider how the outside rooms are configured. (See The Solutions on the next page.)

Consider using skylights in your remodeled space. Obviously, this is not always an option. Nor are they necessarily easy to install correctly on an existing roof. But there is nothing more pleasing than natural light from above, especially in a small, intimate room. If possible, install a *skylight pipeline*; this delivers natural light to different locations using just one skylight.

Not all light is natural. Your use of interior lighting is also important. If you plan to remove interior walls or ceilings (or can get access to the ceiling and walls through the efforts of a skilled electrician), adding general and specific purpose lighting is relatively inexpensive, but offers big benefits. The more lighting options you can add, the better the overall effect.

Once the walls or ceiling are open, it does not cost a great deal to be generous with the lighting fixtures. Dimmers are essential to manage your light needs (individual dimmers do not cost much more than the basic switch).

The Solutions

Traditional windows may work well for you, but some situations call for a different kind of window. Say you want to introduce more light into a room, but the window placement would mean looking into a neighbor's house or an unattractive view or the loss of privacy. The solution–create a series of smaller windows higher on the wall, and enjoy the light without seeing out and being seen.

Glass blocks have made a huge comeback, particularly in more contemporary homes and in lofts with an industrial look. They can make wonderful interior walls, separating part of a home office from the rest of the living space. The glass wall allows light to filter to a spot in the home that may be dark or underused.

Privacy and a light-filled room are not incompatible if you use shutters on the lower half of large windows, leaving the upper portion exposed to sun and light. Similarly, simple duet shades that move from the bottom up allow half the window to be screened. There are many more simple tricks that are inexpensive and allow a room to be open and airy.

Consider using French doors rather than windows, especially if the location leads to the deck or yard. Nowadays, these kinds of doors offer all the features that safety-conscious consumers demand, and afford a great sense of openness. French doors can be used in interior rooms; like glass block walls, they allow light to filter to the deepest recesses of the house and can be closed to keep out noise.

Try coordinating window placement with shrubs and trees in the garden. Assume that your remodeling has opened up your house's east and south walls, allowing maximum light and sun in the winter. During summer, however, these windows will overheat the room. This is the ideal scenario for the placement of a series of deciduous trees. During summer, they shade the room; in the winter, they are leafless, and let through maximum sunlight. Further, a screen of dense evergreens at the end of the property will not only maintain privacy but also serve as a wind barrier.

On the opposite walls and any new, interior spaces, washing the upper walls and ceiling with soft halogen lighting, hidden behind cove molding (naturally, on dimmers), will balance the light in the room during the day and make it seem open and larger at night. Pin spots, picture spots and lamps placed strategically throughout the room will complete the space. New systems allow you to program your lighting, changing the mood through a combination of lights and lamps.

Exterior lights can illuminate features of your home and garden. Exterior lighting is especially important for safety and security reasons. Imagine having the front and back of the house lit when you come home after dark—not only a warm welcome, but a safe one.

Simple exterior lighting can enhance the effects of your new garden rooms, illuminating small trees, shrubs, fountains, arbors and trellises. The effects can be superb. When planning outside lighting, be sensitive to the direction of light and the breadth of the beam of light. Neither you nor your neighbors want bright spots shining in the house from the garden. General lighting should come from the top down while specific light should reflect from the bottom up.

The Resources

Shopping at a home supply store will give you a very good idea of the basic windows and glass doors available today. *Visit www.hgtv.com* for a great deal of information on a variety of subjects related to windows and doors.

Residential Lighting: Practical Guide (Wiley, 2003) contains dozens of color photos. The book is written specifically for residential use and for homeowners.

Visit *www.outdoor-lighting-catalog.com* to see a variety of manufacturers and applications for outdoor lighting. This site sells products from some 50 manufacturers and offers competitive prices. (Add in the cost of shipping when comparing prices.) Many of the major home improvement stores have similar products and can arrange installation.

31

What Is Hot in Basement Remodeling?

The Challenge

Many homeowners are old enough to remember the old family rumpus room in the basement. The challenge confronting homeowners in the past was to make this space as functional as possible. This almost always meant coming up with a strategic way to hide the support beams and columns in the room. Part of the basement was kept for storage, laundry and utilities, which meant the obligatory paneled wall to separate living space from the mess behind it.

Well, basements are back. New construction often has the basement built in such a way that it can be finished in the future, with higher ceilings, larger windows and open floor plans. A big motivation for rediscovering the basement is that you do not have to build outside the original footprint of the house, and there can be immediate space and living benefits for a relatively small investment.

This chapter addresses how best to use the basement, how to improve access to the renovated room and how to ensure that the results are on budget. While the basic reconstruction of basement space is not necessarily difficult, there are special issues.

The Facts

Typically, the older the home, the more challenging the use of basement space can be. A cellar from the 1920s was never designed to be a family room or home office. In such cases, the first renovation will easily be the most difficult–a lot needs to be removed and there is a lot of cleaning to be done.

Space improved as the housing market changed during the 20th century. Less space was used for the basics and more was available for other purposes. Nevertheless, the basement was often divided and the ceiling height limited by ductwork and support beams. Stairs, never intended for frequent use, tended to be steep.

No matter the era, certain basement features are inherent to all housing and must be taken into account before you attempt renovation:

- House foundations and the flooring in the basement vary greatly. Some are cement footings with block or brick walls. Others are poured concrete, with some brick above ground.
- Standards for cement floors are not consistent. Some old homes still have dirt floors or a very thin veneer of cement. This raises the issue of moisture and the inevitable foundation leaks and subsequent problems with mold and mildew.
- Floors and walls are uneven. This space frequently may not have been designed for living, so the standards and tolerances are quite different.
- At the time of construction, it did not matter where the builder mounted electrical boxes or gas and water meters, but their location may not fit your current plans. Ceilings and the cavity in the floors can be filled with conduit, heating ducts, water pipes and bell wire.

The Solutions

First, get rid of moisture. This may require sealing the walls and floors from the inside and possibly even from the outside—a very expensive proposition. Specialty contractors will help and will guarantee their work. Nevertheless, there is always the risk of water of some kind, whether flood or seepage. Vapor barriers on the floors and walls are essential. So, too, is insulation.

Basements are perfect environments for man-made materials. Surfaces that do not absorb moisture are best. Try not to use drapes and wall-to-wall or plush carpeting. A tile floor with area rugs is much easier to clean after water damage.

You may not need an architect, but hiring a designer is worth every penny. The two most common mistakes in basement construction are that they are overbuilt compared to the rest of the house, or that they still look like basements, not real living rooms. The amount of space available will determine how you handle the ultimate design: the more space, the easier it is to define the basement and its relationship to the rest of the house.

If the room is large enough, do not view it as one space. That does not mean building all sorts of walls to separate the sitting area from the home office. But you do want to design the space, including the furniture, to match the first floor of your house: different areas for different functions. If the room is too open, the sight lines are confusing. You cannot see your whole first floor from one vantage point, so why should you be able to view this room at a glance? This is why you need a designer.

Overbuilding means using materials and appliances that are substantially better than the rest of your house. If strangers were to walk through your home at an open house, would they consider the basement the prominent room? If so, its position in the house is out of proportion and the resale value of the house will not reflect the cost and detail of this level of finished basement.

On the other hand, do not renovate the basement halfway. Why spend $10,000 and not have a useable, clean and comfortable space, when an additional $4,000 would make it exactly what you want? An example of this problem is provided by a homeowner who developed a very comfortable space. However, the entrance had a heavy door and steep, dark steps, which made the room uninviting. Solve your entrance and exit issues before starting on the rest of the room. And remember, you also need a second exit from the basement for emergency use.

Use every bit of the room well–including built-in shelves, cabinets and modular dividers–so that more than one activity can take place and each space is clearly defined. Separate utility and storage areas from living space. Make the room(s) environmentally friendly. Light and conditioned air are two of the most important features of a quality room.

If the windows are small, consider making them bigger. Artificial light, if placed correctly, can make a huge difference and give you a sense of quality space–strong indirect lighting around the perimeter of the room, plenty of lamps and the use of ceiling spots to wash an area or a wall.

Nothing makes a basement feel more like a basement than unconditioned air and windows that cannot open. If security is a concern, install windows that have a limited opening. Avoid glass blocks or iron grates.

If you build a bathroom–and if space allows, you should–there are new exhaust systems to keep it fresh. Simple in-floor heating devices that are not tied into the central heating system make the floor comfortable for everyone.

A major manufacturer offers new wall systems that take the place of traditional studs and drywall. The basement refinishing system is advertised as taking 7 to 10 days to complete. It is moisture-proof, will not warp, is removable if access is needed, offers thermal and noise protection, and can be adapted to any ceiling type or height. It is also advertised as clean, neat and efficient.

Some of the more specific trends in basement remodeling:

- Sheetrock ceilings versus soft tile.
- Open and comfortable access by stairs or directly outside.

- Sophisticated lighting, including under cabinet, spots and cans, all adjustable to soften the effect.
- Light colors on walls, floors and ceilings, making the rooms look larger and brighter.
- Entertainment area with a refrigerator, sink, wine rack or small bar.
- Interior windows that allow light to filter through the entire space–frosted glass, for example, works well and still offers a sense of privacy.
- Pocket or folding doors, when doors are required. Get rid of the large, traditional doors as they take up too much space and are intrusive.
- Media center, including a home theatre (this does not have to cost a fortune).
- Prefinished wood floors with area rugs on the floor.
- Home office or guest bedroom (or a combination of both) with a sliding door to close out the noise.
- Modular walls or dividers to rearrange the space without further construction.
- Built-in fish aquarium–especially colorful salt water installations.

The Resources

Visit *www.servicemagic.com* for additional information and referrals for contractors specializing in basement renovation. If you visit *www.basementideas. com*, you will find a very attractive site where the author has an inexpensive book called *Basement Ideas*; it is sold only as a download. The site shows pictures of finished basements and strong testimonials as to the quality of the information sold.

32

What Is Hot in Kitchen Remodeling?

The Challenge

The kitchen, the kitchen, the kitchen–fast becoming the most repeated words in real estate and home renovation. It is *the* room in the house and is more often than not the primary focus of any major remodeling. Everyone wants the kitchen to shine, and it is the first thing that potential buyers focus on. The kitchen is the hub of the house, where family and friends gather. It is often open to the rest of the house, especially the family room and is the place to show off just a bit. It is also the most expensive room in the home (apart from an addition).

Kitchens are typically the first major renovation project. Homeowners want the best they can afford: up-to-date appliances, and modern convenience and comfort. Remodeling the kitchen is no different than renovating any other part of the house–the project still needs to be on budget and within the standards of the neighborhood. (If there is one room that is overbuilt in relation to the rest of the house, it is the kitchen.)

The Facts

In times past, many wealthy homes often had the food preparation area as an out-building. In more modest homes, the humble hearth was the food preparation area. The fire in the hearth was also the center of the home, if only because it offered heat. Although homeowners do not now flock to the kitchen for this reason, family and friends do show up for good smells and socializing. Kitchens have come full circle!

As today's lifestyles grow faster and less formal, the kitchen has come to mirror the way we live. The room has become more open and inviting, a true family room where it is possible to spend quality time. All the same, it is important to remember that that the kitchen is primarily a workspace.

For the last few decades, most kitchen designs have been based on three standard layouts: the U-shaped kitchen, the L-shaped kitchen and the galley kitchen. All three use the work triangle concept that basically positions the three major kitchen components (refrigerator, stove and sink) in a triangular pattern. This standard was considered to be the most efficient layout in the 1950s, after a research study showed that the room was used mostly by women, profiled as a group who:

- Stayed home during the day.
- Worked alone in the kitchen.
- Cooked most foods from scratch.
- Needed storage space for about 400 items.

Times have changed. More recently, the National Kitchen and Bath Association (NKBA) co-sponsored research that recognized the changing usage patterns in the kitchen. It found that most women now:

- Work outside the home.
- Share the cooking duties with spouse or partner.
- Prepare very few foods from scratch.
- Require storage space for 800 items.

From these trends, industry experts now design kitchens with at least minimum standards for kitchen efficiency, convenience, traffic spaces, distances between items, countertop size and cabinet space.

Design encompasses more than efficiency. It also includes the look of the kitchen in relation to the rest of the house, as well as individual expectations and tastes. Fact is, you have an almost overwhelming task choosing designs to suit your lifestyle. Most homeowners, and the designers and architects working for them, choose from six basic kitchen styles.

Victorian

Usually characterized by pointed-arch windows, elaborate trim, stone or tile floors, simple wall treatments and other Gothic details. Light fixtures range from chandeliers to astrals and sconces. Cabinets are usually weathered-looking and made of real, heavy wood with chrome pulls and knobs.

Modern

Most recent designs include sleek, straight and clean lines. Less is more: fewer accessories, visible appliances and details. Common materials include stainless steel, marble, granite and frosted glass. Basic geometric shapes and bold, bright colors such as reds, blues and yellow, and black and white, are prevalent.

Southwestern

A lot of detail and craftsmanship. Natural materials such as stucco and hand-painted fabrics are very common, as are wood, quarry tile, ceramic tile, earth tones and bold accessories. Colors reflect the nature of a desert—warm oranges, greens, tans and browns incorporating ceramic materials and terra cotta.

Traditional

This style plays up architectural details such as crown moldings, raised wood paneling and rich, deep colors to enhance the mood. Dark stains, honey tones, semi-opaque paints, wicker baskets and oak cabinets add to a formal feel.

Eclectic

This style is not characterized by a particular color palette, patterns, style or material, but is a mix of decorations from numerous eras, including hand-me-downs, second-hand items and other recyclables. Kitchens range from modern appliances mixed with antique decorations to the exact opposite.

Country

Rustic, weathered look creates a warm, cozy feeling in a country-style home. Colors range from muted hues to earth tones. Exposed beams, pine paneling, brick and barn boards are elements used to express this style. Fabrics and patterns are a sure way to create a country feeling, as is the use of wallpaper and baskets.

Despite all the choices, it appears that most people prefer some combination of traditional styling. That said, homeowners really are in the business of renovating kitchens to reflect their own lifestyles and interests.

The Solutions

Your first concern is to determine which style is right for you and how you will use the kitchen. From these decisions, all other matters follow. Because of the costs involved, kitchen renovations typically require professional help.

More than ever, the kitchen space is likely to be open. It is therefore important to match its design with the furniture and color scheme of the rest of the house. For example, you might use the same flooring throughout the first floor. Consider choosing cabinets that look more like furniture and pick a pattern that complements your overall decorating scheme.

The larger the kitchen, the easier it is to outfit it for a modern family. Most kitchens, however, are not as large as homeowners want, and unless an addition is contemplated, it is a difficult to get it all in. The trick is to find additional square footage you did not realize you had. Remove a wall, expose a closet or raise the ceiling. Carefully plan your cabinetry for items exclusive to the kitchen. Why create a cabinet for cleaning supplies when you store them elsewhere in the house?

Cabinets will probably be the most expensive element in your kitchen (up to 50 percent of your budget). They also use the most space and largely set the prevalent style and tone. You can include a huge array of features and accessories, including sliding shelves, Lazy Susans, swing-out spice racks and pull-outs. Also consider different moldings to reinforce the fine quality of the cabinetry and further match them to the rest of your décor.

Appliances are the next most expensive items (up to 30 percent of costs). Choose them carefully, looking for features you absolutely must have. Some of the features available include:

- Refrigerators with independent temperature ranges within one unit.
- Pull-out drawers in refrigerators.
- Professional electric stoves, where no gas is available.
- Smaller dishwashers.
- Heavy gas cooktops with six to eight burners and big grills.
- Halogen or smooth-top cooktops.
- Double ovens with convection cooking.
- Fast-cooking ovens (work almost at microwave speed but still brown).

Trends are hardly limited to cabinets and appliances. Here is a very modest list of other options:

- Cast-iron sinks in colors other than white.
- Natural quartz that has the look of leather, with built in antimicrobe protection.
- Lyptus wood–for example, mahogany or plantation-grown–for kitchen cabinets.
- Custom-built stainless-steel sinks with a light brushing to hide scratches.
- Composite sinks made of natural stone such as quartz or granite in a resin composite.
- Gold and copper faucets.
- Instant hot water dispensers with an unlimited supply of hot water at a constant temperature of 190°.
- Remote basket strainers to drain your sink.
- Gallery railings around backsplashes, allowing you to hang kitchen items to make them more accessible.
- Granite and stone surfaces for countertops.
- Tinted concrete for floors and countertops.
- Bamboo for floors.
- Rough slate on backsplashes and floors.
- Multiple workstations.
- Built-in wine (or beverage) coolers.

The Resources

Visit *www.homeimprovementportal.com*; this site allows you to check off what you want done. Enter your zip code for a list of local contractors. The major appliance manufacturers all have Websites, so before you shop you can save time and effort by viewing products online.

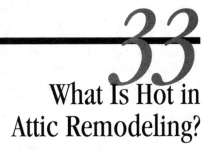

What Is Hot in Attic Remodeling?

The Challenge

The hunt is on for new space; you like your neighborhood and your house, but need room. For some homeowners, the solution is simple: look up. While many newer homes have small spaces above the second (or first) floor living area, there is a huge stock of housing with traditional attic space, often large enough to be built-out without major structural work.

The challenge is how to utilize your upstairs space in a safe, clean and comfortable way—and according to code. Most attics, even large ones, were never intended as living space. Access to the space is limited or non-existent. Fortunate homeowners have stairs to the attic, but they may be small or steep, or have limited head clearance.

The building standards in an attic can be far different from those in the rest of the house. Undersized lumber is typical for the floor joists as well as the structural members holding the roof. While roofs can be heavy, especially if there are several layers of roofing on them, the rafters were sized for a roof only.

All this assumes that your roof supports are conventional rafters and not a truss system. With rafters, you have open space, even with the possibility of an occasional support beam here and there. Trusses, usually used in newer construction, look like a spider web of crisscrossing boards. If you have a trussed room, go to plan B and refinish the basement or add on to the house, because the attic is not available.

If there is a conventional rafter system in the attic, the height of the attic is of special concern. The room is unuseable if you cannot stand comfortably in the middle of the room and move throughout 60 percent to 70 percent of the area without hitting your head. You also have to make some relative judgment as to the usability of the room. A long, narrow room is not much use (except for storage).

Finally, can you find the space on the second floor to add a staircase or at least improve the one you have? This may not be so easy–useable staircases are tricky and require planning for best use and safety.

The Facts

Remodeling magazine reports that the average for converting an attic to about 260 square feet of useable space is just under $36,000. This assumes that you will: add a 15-foot shed dormer (basically, changing the slope of the roof on one side to make it more like a vertical wall); add four windows; finish the walls and carpet the floor; tap into the existing heating and air condition systems; and retain the existing stairs. The good news is that such remodeling will get you back as much as 83 percent of the original cost at sale time (in cities, the rate of return is substantially higher).

Whether you are doing the job yourself or hiring a contractor, you can substantially reduce the cost and complexity of attic conversion if you do not add a dormer or new stairs or substantially rebuild old stairs.

Load bearing walls are extremely important when planning and executing your attic remodeling. The weight of the attic *flows* down through these walls to the foundation. Where and how you stack new walls must be analyzed so that they are not built on non-bearing walls. You will have problems otherwise.

Similarly, floor joists are often undersized in the attic, or are 24 inches on center rather than 16 inches. You will probably have to sister new joists to the existing ones, tying them into the support walls below. If you add 2 x 6s to existing 2 x 4s, then you have raised the floor height just a bit. (Most building codes call for flooring to support 30 pounds per square foot.) This will affect your ceiling height (you still have to add plywood and carpeting or tile). It will also affect the stairs, making the last riser just a bit higher than the others.

Typical requirements when building out your new attic space include:

- Stairway width a minimum of 36 inches.
- Ceiling height of the stairway at six feet, eight inches.
- Step risers about eight inches, all the same height.
- Stair treads at least 10 to 14 inches deep.
- Ceiling height of seven feet, six inches for three-quarters of the attic room.
- Some operating windows.

Your local code will detail the particulars for your area. As a rule, if you cannot meet these minimal standards, the attic space may not be useful after all.

What are the current trends in attic use? Because of its location away from the hustle and bustle of the rest of the house, it can be a very special place for:

- Master bedroom with bath and shower (room permitting).
- Child's play room.
- Library or music room.
- Guest bedroom.
- Hobby or craft room.
- Children's bedroom (although you may not want the noise over head).
- Home theatre, complete with a great sound system.
- Second family room (a frequent request from homeowners).
- Exercise room (just getting the equipment up there will keep you in shape).
- Game room (pool tables come apart for delivery).

The Solutions

Embrace the permit process in this particular remodeling effort. Learn and understand the permitted limits on height, weight, electrical work, heating and air conditioning. You will need drawings of the attic space and of the house itself, and a detailed description of the foundation. You may have to have a structural engineer advise you on weight limits on your foundation.

Make the entrance and stairs as accessible and efficient as possible. If the flow to the attic room is terrible, the room will not be used. If the stair's risers are of non-standard height and tread, the stairs may need to be rebuilt. Consider a circular staircase–they come in a variety of widths and are custom made to your space. You can even get hardwood flooring (or carpeting) to fit on the metal treads, or simply keep it clean and simple and use it as is. You must have sufficient headroom to move freely (and remember–you will need to move materials, furniture and fixtures up these stairs during and after construction).

Some attics were divided into small rooms years ago, but this does not work with today's lifestyle and living needs. Take these rooms out and start again; you will also be ensuring that the work will be done to current code.

Plan early for the introduction of electrical service, HVAC and plumbing. Ideally, you would like to tie into existing systems, but that may not always be easy (a bathroom will have to be situated above current stacks and water lines; otherwise it would be prohibitively expensive and could scuttle the entire remodeling).

Consider a wall air conditioning unit rather than expanding the in-house duct system to the attic. The same is true with heating. Your furnace might not be large enough to comfortably heat the air three stories up. In any case, heat rises, and since the entrance to the room will be through an open stairwell, your heating needs may be rather simple, assuming the walls are sufficiently insulated.

To stop it from getting *too* hot in an attic bedroom, a skylight that can be opened or vented may be a huge help in reducing the heat. Positioned above the open stairs, it acts like a chimney, taking the hot air right out of the room. Skylights in general provide great natural light and the open look will make the room seem much bigger. If installed properly, they will not leak.

Plan your furniture needs carefully. You may not be able to get the big-screen TV up the stairs to the new attic space. (Flat-screen technology can come to the rescue, but at a much higher price!) Furniture that can be assembled in place might be a necessary compromise.

The Resources

There are a number of books devoted to attics exclusively. Consider *Attics: Your Guide to Planning and Remodeling* (Better Homes and Gardens, 1999). This is a short, simple book with lots of photos and examples. It clearly shares the view that the new attic space should be as good as any in your house!

Attics, Dormers and Skylights–For Pros by Pros (Taunton, 2005) is a book for those who might take on attic construction themselves. Specific projects are discussed and explained with illustrations. All the important attic remodeling issues are covered efficiently and clearly.

34

What Is Hot in Bathroom Remodeling?

The Challenge

The bathroom is no longer a simple, small functional space. Certainly, a downstairs powder room retains these basic features, but when it comes to the children's or guest bath, bathrooms move up in status and quality substantially. However, nothing can compare with the trends in master baths (often part of a larger master suite). This is a whole new world of space, luxury, function and comfort. The new master bath can be the size of a bedroom and have the look and feel of an expensive hotel. And homeowners are willing to pay for all the amenities.

Most older homes did not have multiple bathrooms when they were built, but homeowners today want baths on every level of the house. Parents do not want to share a bath with the kids and often the kids do not want to share a bath with each other. Three and one-half baths are the minimum in most new houses.

Where do you find the space to expand or even add a master bath? If you are planning to add a two-story addition, the entire second level of the new construction can be devoted to the master suite. Tie it into the existing bedroom (which then could become a bath and dressing room/closet), and you have the footprint for a magnificent room. Of course, the cost is enormous, and it may not be in your budget or your plans.

Your challenge is to look at your home differently. Creative space management may allow you to expand or add a bath, but will mean taking from Peter to give to Paul: a house with five bedrooms becomes a house with a master and three smaller bedrooms; part of the hallway or other common area can be borrowed for the new bathroom (so, too, can closets); and making the master bedroom smaller, as well as taking some space from an adjoining room, might also work.

The Facts

The costs for remodeling a master bathroom vary wildly. A huge room, built into new space, with all the latest goodies in the best materials with *his* and *her* everything could easily surpass $75,000.

Consider a more modest proposal, expanding a current five- by seven-foot room to nine by nine. All the fixtures are relocated and a substantial shower is included. The toilet is set up in its own room and a bidet is added. Also added are a custom vanity with medium-range tops, and undermount sinks with quality faucets. The floor is ceramic tile, the walls are papered and hard-wood trim is part of the finish. General lighting is added. *Remodeling on Line* reports that this midrange renovation would cost $11,000–$26,000 if using upper-range materials.

The sample above is merely the starting point. Luxury is not the only issue you face; there are basic and practical issues you need to consider:

- Without storage, your new room will look cluttered.
- How much natural light do you have and how can you add more? If a skylight is an option, great; if not, the larger the window(s) the better.
- The shower door should swing into the bathroom, not into the shower itself.
- Code and common sense dictate that you have ground fault interrupters on all electrical outlets, reducing the possibility of shock or worse.
- Place all electrical switches away from the tub or shower.
- Most codes require that you use temperature- and pressure-balanced water control valves.
- Hydrotherapy is popular, and is also practical and important if you suffer from arthritis or stress.
- If you envisage staying in the house into your middle age (or older), plan on adapting the room to your future needs.

Understand the need for careful spacing between and around fixtures and tubs. Most master bathrooms are designed for two people, so think carefully about dimensions within the room. You also have to clean this room, so access is important:

- Allow 15 inches from the center of the toilet to the wall.
- Place double vanities so that they are 20 inches apart, edge to edge.
- Ensure that there is at least 30 square inches of clear floor space in front of a toilet or bidet.
- The shower stall size should be at least 34 square inches.
- How big a tub do you need? The only way to know is get into the sample and see if you fit and are comfortable.

- Allow 30 inches along the length of tub for space to get in and out comfortably.
- The bathroom door must swing so that it does not interfere with people in front of fixtures.
- The space must be comfortable for two people at the same time.

Put away practicality for the moment and think about some of the great new features that homeowners want in the master bath:

- Being warm and comfortable are top of the list—install new radiant heating systems for the floor that are independent of your whole-house HVAC system.
- A towel warmer.
- Hi-fi and television for entertainment while soaking.
- The largest and deepest tub you can include (making sure that it is well supported, as it will be very heavy when filled).
- Fog-free windows and mirrors.
- Flooring and walls in natural stone, marble and a host of new man-made materials.
- Windows that block the view from the outside with a touch of the finger.
- New, electronic toilets with warm water hygiene and air freshening features.
- Faux-wall finishes and highly stylized cabinets.

The Solutions

Because storage is so important, one homeowner has added to the bathroom, but kept the original footprint and walls. The storage is an ante-room to the bathroom, with the door removed. To make the space work even better, the door swings out into the bedroom. Both sides of the addition are lined with shelves and drawers. The new walls are painted and finished exactly as the rest of the bedroom. A flat-screen television has been added on the outside wall, facing the bed.

Try to understand where storage needs to be in relation to a specific task. Keep towels within easy reach of the shower or sink. If you run out of shampoo, you do not want to walk the length of the bathroom to find more. Have a place for everything. A bathroom looks terrible when bottles and boxes are stored in the open, on top of the toilet or on the window shelf.

Consider spending a bit more for both general and mood lighting. Yes, you need sufficient brightness to put on makeup or shave, but who wants glaring light first thing in the morning or while taking a relaxing bath or shower? Separate the lighting with different switches and add those dimmers!

Ensure better access and personal comfort as you age by adding and changing features in your master bathroom:

- Widen the doorway to make it wheelchair-accessible—and that includes the shower door.
- Buy toilets that are higher than standard models.
- Limit thresholds into the room and into the shower.
- Grab bars are a must in the shower and a good idea in other areas of the bathroom.
- Quality flooring can be non-slip—a good decision at any stage of life.
- New tubs make it easier to get in and out of the bath.
- Include a bench or seat in the shower.

Within reason, personalize your bathroom with permanent changes, such as walls and fixtures. If room permits, add an antique chest of drawers for towels and linens. Enhance the look of the room with old shaving mugs, exotic perfume bottles or small prints or reproductions.

The judicious use of mirrors can make the room seem brighter and larger. Lighten the walls and cabinets with colors that do not make the room seem constricted. If you have an interesting design feature in the bathroom—for example, a high ceiling—draw attention to it. Add lights that shine up onto the ceiling or use a fine wood or paneling on the ceiling itself.

Be creative in your tile selection; you can add color and unusual features at relatively little cost. Most designers and stores selling upscale tiles or marble will show you design and pattern books from which you can choose a variety of combinations.

The Resources

For a good selection of products and advice, visit *www.abathroomguide.com* or *www.directbathroomremodeling.com*. If you plan to do some or all of the work yourself, visit *www.doityourself.com*. Finally, a new, user-friendly tub concept for older homeowners can be found at *www.tubcut.com*.

35

What Is Hot in Backyard Remodeling?

The Challenge

One the fastest-growing trends in the country is refashioning the backyard to be an extension of the home. This is not about common backyard improvements but the creation of living spaces for various activities, from entertaining to meditation.

Creating these spaces is not necessarily easy. The average homeowner looks at the backyard and has a hard time imagining what it might look after radical changes. Radical does not necessarily meaning tearing out everything or not having any green space at all, but rethinking the role of the yard in terms of lifestyle, maintenance and personal interests.

Visualize your property as an extension of your home. The plans can be grand (and expensive) or they can be simpler and more natural. While you may do some of the work yourself, a professional designer or landscape architect should at least help with the master plan.

The work involved can be back-breaking and challenging. Space may be small or access limited, meaning that heavy equipment cannot be used. Instead, picks, shovels and wheel barrels become necessary. You also have to decide if you want to do the entire job in one season or over 2 or 3 years.

The most important reason to do the work is to increase your personal satisfaction and enjoyment. However, by some estimates, good landscaping can also increase the value of your home by up to 15 percent. Consider what real estate agents call *curb appeal*. It involves not only the house, but how it is framed with fences, trees, trellises, shrubs and flowers.

Finally, what do you want the space or spaces to be? Do you need to balance social commitments with your desire for a simple, natural space? What about children's play areas versus a more formal design? Where can you make the best use of space? Are there safety issues, such as small children and an open in-ground pool?

The Facts

There has been a 4 percent drop in sales of gardening products in each of the last 2 years. The reason might be that the boomers are getting older and less able to take on large, complicated gardens. At the same time, younger people are more attuned to hobbies involving technology and computers, and less interested in outside activities.

An important trend is the desire by both groups for someone *else* to do the work. Further, boomers are making their gardens and landscaping less work-intensive. They are taking out the long rows of perennial garden beds that require considerable labor, and replacing them with more work-friendly spaces with native grasses, flowering shrubs, evergreens and ornamental trees.

Container gardening is becoming very popular. A yard, patio or deck can be peppered with flowers, shrubs and evergreens in containers. Once established, container gardening is easy on the back, work schedule and wallet. You can still do-it-yourself, but have time for other activities–like doing absolutely nothing!

If front and back gardens are to flow together, both spaces should have similar design features. However, if they are separated from each other or there is small or limited access between them, you can have two very different spaces without conflict.

While many homeowners desire the perfect lawn, easy-to-care-for alternatives are making headway. Grass takes time, effort and lots of water. Landscaped areas often use ground cover, ivy, bark and stone in place of sod. Native materials are especially common in the Southwest, where it is difficult to grow some traditional backyard favorites.

Water, water everywhere…this is the single biggest trend in the last decade. Small space or large, there is always room for a fountain, running stream or koi pond. Water is soothing, adds focus to a landscape and can block out unwanted noise. Fountains and pools do require some work; some of it messy. They have to be cleaned and closed (in areas with cold winters). And if you want your pond to be something other than a green, soggy mess, learn how to use the filtration system. Water plants can influence the look of your pond and ease its maintenance.

Standing water is a problem. Yards have low spots where water accumulates and threatens the house's foundation or basement. Getting rid of too much water is a priority before any further work is done. Dry streams or French drains can carry the water away to the street or city sewers.

Landscapers and designers focus on five aspects of outdoor space:

Color: The strong colors like red, more secondary like violet, a mix of the two, and finally neutral colors like gray and white.

Form: Often expressed in terms of the shape of plants and objects.

Lines: How the eye passes over the space–the flow or movement from one area to another.

Scale: Are plants and other fixtures in proportion to the house, trees and outbuildings–and to each other?

Textures: A combination of coarse (gravel or bark), medium (stone) or fine (sand or tightly clipped grass).

The trick is to get these aspects coordinated with each other and with the space that is being designed. This is not easy–harmonizing flowers, hardscape and shrubs can take time and practice. However, if you do not like where you planted the lilac bush, you can simply move it or trim it back.

The Solutions

Before you dig, you *must* call the local utilities and ask them to mark water, gas, phone and power lines. Insist that this service is part of the written agreement with your contractor. As a rule, the marking service is free, and the local utilities are happy to help.

Most designers will tell you that curved lines and multiple repetitions make the yard look natural (unless your plan calls for a formal, edged European look). Repetition of some of the same plants and colors throughout the space will help unify it. Smaller plants should be used in groupings of three or five–never even numbers and never in a straight row.

Do not build your outdoor spaces piecemeal; that is why the master plan is so important. This does not mean that you cannot spread the work over time. It is easier to think about your space in spring or summer, when everything is lush. The real trick is to make it attractive in the fall and winter, with fall color, grasses, evergreens and interesting shapes.

If you have large shade trees, do not plant sun-hungry border gardens. There are many alternatives, including using the canopy of trees as the *roof* over a secluded space for reading or relaxation. If the soil is hard clay, work in compost; but realize that you will have to limit your selection of plant materials. The same applies for sandy soil, hot or dry conditions, hillsides and more.

Privacy is important. Some communities prohibit fences that block views (or any fence at all, for that matter). However, you can plant natural screens of evergreens and deciduous trees. Structures like arbors and trellises can define the space, as well as enhance its beauty and privacy. Protection from the sun in the summer is crucial–situate cooking and dining areas in the shade. Large arbors filled with vines can give the space an intimacy and coolness that will be welcome in the summer.

Cooking areas are all the rage. If such an area is near the kitchen or family room, the space literally flows into the backyard. The space can be defined by a deck, stained concrete or natural stone or slate. Your choices of color should blend with the house and the rest of the space. Whatever your choice of hardscape, soften it with planters, shrubs, small flower beds or a water feature.

The largest expanse of hardscape is often the driveway. If you replace it, consider staining it to match the house and the rest of your plan. More expensive alternatives include stone or brick. In some regions, crushed stone, gravel or even oyster shells are an attractive, softer alternative.

To create more space, consider taking out old, unattractive trees, leveling steep terrain or removing a hill. All require professional help, careful attention to water and soil erosion, and typically need permits. They also cost a lot of money, but may well be worth it.

The Resources

At *www.mydesignscape.com*, you can purchase the online services of a professional landscape designer. You can receive sample CAD/CAM designs and interact with the designer to complete the process. Take your final plans to your contractor, and away you go. Visit *www.homeandgardentreasures.com* for interesting products, including fountains, plant material and yard art.

What Is Hot in Garages?

The Challenge

Garages are fast becoming all the rage in home building and renovation. It is not uncommon for a new or renovated house to have a garage with at least three stalls and extra room for storage. Many homeowners would love the same kind of open space, and the flexibility to use a garage for more than just cars.

In some cases, remodelers want to use the space afforded by an attached garage as extra living space. The cost of renovation in comparison to building an addition, remodeling an older basement or upgrading the attic can be very competitive. Part of the challenge, however, is to make it look like a living space, both inside and out.

You may want to change or renovate a garage simply because your car or cars do not fit into the existing space. Many of today's larger vehicles were never intended to fit into a 50-year old garage. Often, the height of the garage is a problem, limiting the size of car, as well as preventing use of the ceiling or rafter space for accessible storage.

Finally, garages today reflect contemporary values and lifestyles. People are tired of dirty, greasy garages, with clutter and junk surrounding the cars. They crave organization, convenience and order. Your challenge is to determine what you need and how best to use the garage space to accomplish your goals.

The Facts

Begin with the idea that you are looking for space within the original footprint of the house. The garage is an ideal candidate for conversion to a laundry room/mud room, music studio, home theatre, home office, workshop, art studio or even an extension of the kitchen or family room. A great advantage of converting an attached garage is that it is on the ground floor, ideal if you are planning on living in your home as you age.

Builders and architects estimate that remodeling a garage into living space can cost from $25 to $100 per square foot. This compares very favorably to remodeling the rest of the house. While cost-effective, improving garages is often not as easy as it sounds. Garages were not built to be made into living space. Their poured concrete floors are often thin, and can be cracked and soiled after years of use. Walls tend to be underbuilt, with little insulation. In addition, garages tend to have no heating, water or plumbing.

You may find that building above the attached garage is a sensible and affordable way to add value and room. Assuming that the foundation will bear a second floor, this renovation could be ideal. The trick is to build the addition in keeping with the house, as well as to make access to the new space functional. Nothing is worse than a room that flows into another room or a tandem room; you need to plan and integrate the old second-floor bedroom with the new, above-garage addition.

If you want to keep the garage as basically a garage, the hot trend is to maximize space and use the garage, or part of it, for storage or hobbies and still retain it as a place to keep cars.

The Solutions

If you convert a garage into living space, you may still need a place to park cars and store yard supplies. Building an unattached garage, perhaps with an enclosed breezeway to the house, may be a relatively inexpensive solution. There are construction companies that specialize in building garages to your specifications. Of course, you will need enough space, the necessary permits and a plan of how you are going to route traffic to and from the garage.

Building an unattached garage is an ideal opportunity to redesign your backyard and bring your landscaping plan up to date. This is the perfect time to replace your old, dated driveway with brick, stone or any of the new stained concrete applications. Further, remember that you need to maintain easy access to the house and the rest of the yard–including decks, pools and patios.

An innovative use of an old, small garage is to retrofit it into a greenhouse. This means removing the roof and installing operating skylights or an actual greenhouse glass roof with vents for releasing heat. If there are windows, you can expand their size and introduce quality, double-paned functioning lights. If your garage does not have an operating drain, consider installing a French drain–a simple well with a barrel and stone in it, and holes in the bottom to allow water to leach out. The best part of this conversion is that the walls and floors do not need much work, as this is a room where water and dirt will be welcome.

You may decide to keep the garage as a garage, but want to add features that make it cleaner, neater and more useable. Consider the new garage systems that wrap around the room and allows for workbenches, storage and decent flooring. These systems are expensive and require quite a bit of preparation. Most of the components hang on a series of horizontal wall panels that require a substantial commitment of time and money, assuming that you are doing it yourself.

That said, making a garage neat and clean need not be prohibitively expensive. Consider using simple hanging brackets for garden tools, lawn chairs and children's toys. Lighting is an important issue if you want to use the garage for more than just cars. Inexpensive, easy-to-install hanging fixtures can make dark corners useful and useable.

If the garage is not long or wide enough to accommodate your storage and remodeling plans, consider adding a bump-out or shed addition. The trick is to make it look as though it was part of the garage and house in the first place. It needs to be sturdy, dry and insulated, and should include windows and good lighting. Any addition should of course comply with current code in terms of foundation, flooring, height and length. If you are opening up the side or end of the garage, make sure that the original structure has the proper headers to bear the weight of the walls and roof above.

Do not build onto the garage if you do not have sufficient headroom. And remember—the garage door has to go somewhere. Be realistic about what benefits you get from adding on. It might be better to tear down and start all over.

If it is not feasible to take down the garage or remodel it for storage and other use, consider building a separate storage shed. As a rule, the storage buildings available as a kit from the home improvement store are inexpensive, have built-in flooring and are accepted by most communities as a reasonable addition to yards. However, many of the designs are not very attractive. Choose carefully and buy a larger structure than you think you need; the space will always come in handy.

You may find a prefabricated building that serves your needs in terms of space and cost, but decide that you do not like the exterior look. Paint and a bit of landscaping are wonderful and inexpensive solutions to this problem. If you do not like the prefabricated storage sheds, there are plenty of examples of storage/ potting sheds in the home magazines and on cable TV.

One of the best ways to improve your garage and its functionality is to drag everything out and start throwing or giving it away. There is the age-old, quaint custom called a garage sale, whereby you pass your current junk to a neighbor so that it can now be his junk. If you do not want a garage sale, consider selling items on eBay. If you throw stuff out, try to recycle as much as possible. And if you must keep something, consider off-site storage.

The Resources

While GarageTek is not the only manufacturer of garage wall, floor and cabinet systems, it is representative of what is available in a mid-price range. These same kinds of systems can be purchased at most major home supply stores. Visit *www.garagetek.com* for more information.

A popular book on the subject is called *Your Garagenous Zone: Innovative Ideas for the Garage* (Paragon Garage Company, 2004). It is a fairly short paperback that takes you through all the basics and shows examples of what can be done. Also consider *Garage: Reinventing the Place We Park* (Taunton, 2003), which describes unusual uses for, as well as the history of, garages.

37

What Is Hot in Home Office Remodeling?

The Challenge

The home office was once simply a place where you paid some bills or surfed the Web.

There is a difference between what you need and what you want. And not only the budget is important—the home office environment needs to reflect the reality of the situation. If it is used just occasionally, the expense and trouble of an elaborate layout probably cannot be justified. However, if the home office is truly a place of business, used 30 or more hours per week, it should be pleasant and reasonably comfortable.

Also, some homeowners who work at home need to entertain or meet clients. This can present a problem if there is not a separate entrance for the office suite. If this need exists, it reduces your options as to where to place the office.

The Facts

IDC Research in Framingham, Mass. estimates that some 33 million people in the United States do income-generating work from home. This number will continue to grow. Some of the 33 million are running home-based businesses, some use their offices even though they are employed full-time and many use the office to complete work over the weekend.

Real estate agents report that home offices are a must for many homebuyers. Companies can cut costs by allowing workers to be based from home, even offering to subsidize the expense of the office. Allowances can be as high as $1,000 per month to cover office supplies, travel and telephone/ Internet connections.

While home offices are all the rage, you may want to consider other options. It is easy to start working at home; it is far more difficult to sustain your momentum and not get distracted by home activities. The best advice is that before you spend

$10,000 to convert a bedroom, try a simpler arrangement in that same room and see if working full-time at home is for you.

One homeowner reports that his business began by sharing his wife's office (she worked out of the house during the day). He found that in the evening when he wanted to work more, they crowded each other. He moved the office to the bedroom, but found it cramped. Then he tried a section of the basement, but the family room was right above the office and it could get very noisy. Finally, the office was built above the garage—a large, bright space with a vaulted ceiling, easy access across the deck from the house, a short commute and a separate entrance for an assistant and visitors. The main point is that the office became a *destination*, out of the house itself.

If you plan to add or convert a room for a home office, expect to pay around $11,000 for a decent-sized space (the size of a small bedroom). *Remodeling* magazine reports that you can expect to get about 55 percent of your investment back if you sell your home. (Of all the possible renovations projects that pay back, the home office is rather low on the list. This seems to contradict those who say that the home office is in high demand. The contradiction may be explained by the fact that buyers assume that the house has a home office and is built into the asking price.)

The main issues to address when designing a comfortable and useful home office are:

- Privacy.
- Efficient equipment layout.
- Good lighting.
- Adequate storage.
- Sufficient phone lines.

The most common places for the home office are bedrooms (first), attics, basements, sunrooms, alcoves on landings and the garage. Remodeling experts recommend avoiding the garage if possible; this kind of reuse requires zoning changes and considerable work and expense to bring the space up to interior living standards. And visitors will always know that your office was your garage; it is not easy to disguise the outside look and get rid of the smell of oil and gas. The resale value of a garage made into an office is virtually nil.

The Solutions

A home office works best if it is a separate room or is located away from living space. A bedroom is an easy solution, as the door can be closed and the work environment segregated from the rest of the home. Part of the basement, assuming it is suitable, can be quite convenient and may even offer its own entrance for people to come and go without going through the house. However, it must be walled off from the rest of the room(s); if the pool table and large-screen TV are also in the basement, do not expect a simple screen or barrier to work. It will not.

Where you place the office is important. Many people need quiet, so it must be located as far away as possible from home activities–in an attic, the far side of the basement, above the garage or a back bedroom. But other needs should be recognized as well. What if you have children at home? In this case, screening off part of the family room or kitchen may be your solution.

Quality lighting is essential. If the room does not have a working window, consider installing one (plus, if possible, a skylight). Install good, general lighting–especially task lighting above frequently used stations. Put them on dimmer switches so you can change the mood and brightness of the room.

If you are converting an existing space, use more than the standard two-plug outlets. Consider adding multiple quad outlets to accommodate lights and equipment. Try to have a separate circuit specifically dedicated to the office. A small television, radio or stereo will allow some background noise without intruding on your work. Forget a fireplace. It is distracting and expensive. You will need more than one phone line, but three is probably excessive in most applications. A simple splitter on the office line will allow you to use the phone and the Internet simultaneously.

If you plan to set up a home office (especially for full-time work), you need to know what, if any, limits local government may place on you–in terms of what you can do in that office, how many people can work there or even whether the office is allowed by current zoning.

You can get the best use of limited space by installing built-in or semi-custom office systems that include cabinets, file drawers, flat work space, a computing station, garages for printers, space to hang coats and more. The sophistication and and cost of the look should be determined by your budget. In any case, vertical storage against the wall is a must.

Bathrooms are a challenge, especially if you have colleagues or clients coming to the office. Ideally, you would like to have a dedicated room as part of your office space. A home office in the basement, with its own entrance, could easily accommodate a small bathroom as part of the suite. In other parts of the house, adding an office bathroom is neither easy nor cheap.

If your new office space is near or open to the rest of the house, install folding or pocket doors that are translucent; they allow light to filter through the rest of the living area but offer privacy. Free-standing screens can provide limited privacy. They do nothing against noise, however.

The Resources

Visit the *Better Homes and Garden* Website at *www.bhg.com* to find an easy-to-use device for planning your office (or other) space. The free design system is called *Arrange-a-Room*; simply drag images to set up the room to see how it will look.

If you use your home office regularly and exclusively for business purposes, you may be entitled to a tax deduction for the business use of your home and depreciation of your equipment (though there are severe restrictions). Your tax adviser or the Internal Revenue Service will provide the best counsel, but there are several IRS publications that lay out the ground rules in this area. Visit *www.irs.gov* for the following:

- *Publication 529 Miscellaneous Deductions: Home Office, Depreciation* sections
- *Publication 587 Business Use of Your Home*
- *Publication 534 Depreciation*
- *Publication 946 How to Begin Depreciating Your Property*

38

What Is Hot in Master Bedroom Remodeling?

The Challenge

Nearly every new subdivision or custom-built home has a list of features, not the least of which is the master bedroom suite. People with older homes watch in envy as every possible feature and function are added to the master. Even if you are adding a major addition to the house, including all the luxuries of new housing is not going to be easy.

When remodeling and trying to improve the master bedroom, the biggest issue is space. Where do you get it and what has to be sacrificed in the process? How large can you make the room, assuming that size is top of the agenda? Can you include extra storage and a bathroom?

The Facts

The primary motivation for remodeling a master bedroom is to create an intimate and comfortable adult space. The master bedroom is the room in which you spend most of your time. It should therefore be comfortable and satisfying.

People with children find that the master bedroom is the one private space in an otherwise public house. It provides an escape from kids, their friends, sleepovers, noise, games and so on–though by necessity there has to be a different set of rules for smaller children

The master suite need not cost that much (though it might not pay for itself when you sell, either–the best estimates indicate a return of only 75 percent of the money expended). A survey by *Remodeling* magazine suggests the average cost of renovating a master bedroom to be about $69,000.

Ideally, the master bedroom should comprise several rooms within a room. It is primarily a place to sleep and get ready for the next day. The majority of the space that is not part of the attached bathroom should be devoted to the bed and bedside furniture, such as tables and lamps. Make this space open, welcoming and relaxing.

The colors, lighting and flooring used in and around the bed area ought to be inviting and an inducement to sleep. Waste a little space, if you have it, to put the bed at an angle. Incorporate windows and add task lighting that allows one person to read while the other can sleep or watch television.

If you have no plans to go beyond the original footprint of the house and you must carve the new master bedroom out of existing space, the obvious choice is to take the space from another bedroom and part of the hallway (if possible). Some older homes have huge hallways and landings, far more than is required. In all cases, if walls are coming down, you and your contractor must know which walls can come down without a header and which are load-bearing (which will need a span or header to keep the building's integrity intact).

When creating rooms within a room, it is essential to have a firm grasp of what you really want–not just something you saw in a magazine. Designers and photographers can make a room look perfect, while in fact it is hugely impractical. For example, say you want the room to function as a reading area as well as an entertainment space. You should be realistic about just how much you will use the space. If you are not a regular reader, the space is wasted.

Besides the creation of more space, popular features of master bedrooms include sitting areas, big closets, dressing areas, snack areas (a small wet bar for morning coffee with a refrigerator) and an entertainment space with a large TV. In some markets, the small wet bar expands to a mini-meal station with built-in cabinets, coffee makers, toasters and small dishwashers, all tucked into a small space. A gas fireplace, built-in stereo with surround systems and specialized lighting round off the list.

How much space is needed for each function? This requires a professional designer. Built-in cabinets and seating can make the room more efficient and create better flow between different areas. One of the biggest mistakes when remodeling the master is adding insufficient closet space. You may be able to accommodate his and her closets, but the main objective is to add as much useable space as possible.

Before embarking on a master bedroom project, you must understand what effect your changes will have at resale. If you eliminate one bedroom in a three bedroom house, is this in keeping with a neighborhood where houses typically have three bedrooms?

In some new constructions, and sometimes in renovated homes, two master bedroom suites are actually built. A first floor plan is created for live-in parents, for whom stairs and other impediments making living upstairs inconvenient. In effect, the room becomes an apartment within the house, perhaps with its own entrance and separate climate control.

The Solutions

If you are adding on to the house, and the master is going to be the second floor of the addition above a family room or garage, access to the new space must flow from the older portion of the house. How are you going to get to the new space? One of the existing bedrooms in the house will probably have to be sacrificed. If this is done well, the house will flow. The old bedroom could be a sitting area or part of the space used for a small, second bath for the rest of the family, complete with washer and dryer.

Insulate not only the walls and ceilings, but also the floor. What good is the new retreat if noise carries up from the first floor? Sound insulation is cheap and well worth it. The same goes for interior walls abutting other bedrooms or common areas near the master bedroom.

If two people share the master, design the room so that the closets and the bath are on one side of the room—a dressing suite. It makes moving about the room easier and there is less chance of disturbing a partner who might still be sleeping. Separate lighting is also important in this arrangement; dimmers and task lighting make it more accommodating and spouse-friendly.

Flooring is a big issue. While almost everyone likes the look of wood or stone, they can be cold on the feet. Some combination of hard surfaces and carpeting or rugs is most comfortable. Also, consider under-floor radiant heating—especially appreciated in the bathroom.

When creating the master bedroom space, make sure that you back up to a wall that has water lines, drains and vents. In new construction, functional rooms requiring water and drainage are almost always stacked one on top of the other or next to each other in order to share plumbing. Your cost for the master renovation will soar if you cannot get ready access to plumbing, heating and vent lines.

Master bedrooms do not always have to be on the second floor. In fact, consider using the attic for the master. You will not only have a fairly large space, but also great views above the trees, privacy from the rest of the house and a real sense of retreat. Naturally, attics have their challenges (see Chapter 33, *What Is Hot in Attic Remodeling?*)

If you plan to live in the house for a longer time, consider putting your master bedroom on the first floor. While very disruptive during construction, reconfiguring the first floor increasingly makes sense. It is easier to move materials and supplies in (no stairs) and easier to get the old walls and plaster out. Further, many homes have underutilized space on the first floor (large living and dining rooms, for example) that can be reconfigured to make the master.

As children age and move away, many couples find that the huge family room is wasted space. Think about using some or all of this space for your first-floor master bedroom, complete with wood-burning fireplace and easy access to the kitchen! If you make changes, try not to make too many structural alterations, so that the space can be turned back into a family room (or dining room for that matter) when it comes time to sell. Dry wall and studs are not expensive. Only your imagination limits the possibilities!

The Resources

The magazine racks are filled with home improvement and decorating books that will stimulate your imagination. See what appeals and what does not. Several books on the subject might be useful, including Joan Kohn's *Its Your Bed and Bath: Hundreds of Beautiful Design Ideas* (Bulfinch, 2004) or *Pottery Barn Bedrooms* (Oxmoor House, 2003). Both are available at *www.amazon.com* or *www.barnesnoble.com*.

Remodeling for Ultimate Storage in Mind

The Challenge

Unless your house was built in the last 20 years and is above-average size (over 2,500 square feet of living space), you will likely be looking for more storage space. This is particularly true for average-sized vintage houses built before the 1950s, when people had fewer possessions and clothing, and therefore less need for closets.

Since you are in the process of adding on or renovating an existing space, now is the perfect time to evaluate your short- and long-term storage needs. Do not assume that your current storage needs will be the same in 5 or 10 years. If you have a growing family (or even if you do not), assume you will own more, want to keep more and need to store more. Further, you will want high-quality storage (dry, clean and accessible).

Off-site storage buildings have sprouted up in almost every neighborhood. Such storage may be a fine alternative, especially if items are bulky and many. However, in-house storage space is a high priority for homebuyers, so plan to build as much as you can into those newly renovated parts of your house.

In the course of remodeling, traditional storage areas (basement, attics and garages, for example) are often changed or eliminated. Your challenge is to find the space and apply systems that will allow you to increase your storage.

The Facts

Storage is less a problem for homes built after 1985, when the concept of master bedrooms and related dressing and closet rooms caught on. However, even such houses suffer from some problems. For example, most houses built in the West and South do not have traditional basements. In addition, most garages are still two-car, as opposed to three-car or oversized.

No matter when your house was built, storage for bulky items has always been an issue–bicycles, sports equipment, tools and workbenches, children's toys, out-of-season bedding, yard and garden appliances, and more.

Each part of the house needs defined storage for personal effects related to that space. Why keep everyday clothing in a closet on the first floor when the bedroom is on another?

In general, built-in storage is probably the best overall system to manage your storage needs. If you are constructing new space or altering existing space, build closets across a bedroom wall, even if they cover the existing closet. Use the old closet for seasonal storage and hang the clothes across the new space. Adding bookshelves and space for a TV or audio components will make the storage space look like it was always part of the room.

If used effectively, room dividers and kitchen islands can offer huge amounts of additional storage for everyday articles. Do not make the cabinet space so large that it interferes with sitting and relaxing. Further, ensure that you install doors and drawers on both sides of the built-in fixture. Your reach space in a cabinet is not much more than about two feet. Consider installing large drawers or pull-out shelves within cabinets in order to get better access.

The Solutions

Break down your storage needs into those items you use frequently (once a month, say) and those things that you use annually or not at all. Keep everyday items in the front of the closet, at eye level, in the main drawers and on easy-to-reach shelves. Those things that are not used frequently should be relegated to the top shelves, to the back of the closet, to the basement or attic, or to the space above the rafters in the garage.

There are great closet systems that have been in use for 20 years. When installed, they can double or triple the amount of closet space. Buy them as ready-to-install sets from the home supply store, or call up specialists who will design and built specific systems for your space. If you are handy with a tape measure, hacksaw, drill and screwdriver, installation is fairly easy.

Long before kitchen cabinets, homeowners depended on the kitchen pantry to hold everything from canning jars to food to cleaning supplies and anything else that did not fit elsewhere in the house. Consider building some variation of a pantry. It can be large enough to walk into, or simply a huge cabinet with moveable shelves and Lazy Susans to use every corner of the space.

Use the ceiling of your kitchen or pantry. Large pots and cookware are very attractive decorations, and hanging them near or above the stove opens as much as 10 percent of your cabinet space for other purposes.

Many people design kitchens so that the top row of cabinets sits some way below the ceiling. If space is a real concern, consider adding a third level right to the ceiling. This solution is ideal for the storage of seasonal items, small appliances, secondary sets of dishes, cherished antiques and more. Add in a ladder design that makes access to the top level safe and convenient.

Plan attic and basement remodeling with storage in mind. With the right systems, you can store a great deal, while still improving the space and making it more livable.

Install shelves, with or without doors, along the eaves of the attic space, on both sides. Some of the doors will lead to nearly unfinished space under the eaves for larger objects, such as boxes of Christmas ornaments or books. Others can be refined and defined to fit the décor of the room. They can store books, videos, pictures and a host of decorative and practical items, and yet make the room cozy and pleasant.

Sometimes, it makes better economic sense to use off-site storage. For example, if you had been using your attic or basement for the majority of your storage, and now are remodeling this space, the stuff needs to go somewhere. With some off-site services, a storage unit is delivered to you; you fill it up and lock it; and then it is taken away to a simple, unheated locker. These facilities are widespread, and are generally secure and clean.

One feature making a comeback is the butler's pantry–a mini-kitchen between the main kitchen and the dining room. Years ago they were found only in the best homes, and were used to hide the mess of the kitchen from the view of the guests. They were also used as a space to warm plates and keep dishes hot until served.

Traditionally, the room contained cabinets, storage, perhaps a wine cooler and a small sink. A microwave and even a separate dishwasher designed for fine china and crystal might also be included. The beauty is that the cabinets go right to the ceiling, affording a tremendous amount of space for infrequently used specialty items. It is also a place to store the mess during and after a party.

Smaller versions of a butler's pantry might comprise a simple line of cabinets along one wall in the kitchen, dining or family rooms. This arrangement is ideal if space is limited. If the cabinets match what is in the kitchen, you get a neat, unified look to the open space, while extending your kitchen and storage needs beyond the basic room. Large drawers, no matter where the pantry is situated, are absolutely essential for holding serving platters and other odd-shaped items. Glass doors give the storage unit a furniture-like look, allowing for a display of fine china or crystal.

The price tag for a butler's pantry will vary, but a basic row of fine cabinets with a microwave and wine cooler will not be much more than $3,000 or $4,000, depending on the choice of countertop materials. What the space adds, however, is a permanent, attractive solution to your storage needs.

The Resources

The Do-It-Yourself Network features practical and handy projects that can be done by the average person. Visit *www.diynetwork.com* for information on storage chests and window seats, among other storage projects.

A very good, practical book on the subject of home storage is reviewed at *www.housekeeping.about.com.* Titled *Home Storage Idea Book* (Taughton, 2002), it is divided into seven sections that cover the basics through to specific storage needs for all major areas of the house.

Remodeling to Sell

The Challenge

Let us say you have decided to move to new housing. However, after careful evaluation, you realize that to get top dollar for your house, some changes are going to have to be made. In this situation, your only motivation to remodel is to get your top asking price and move on. This requires a different strategy, a different discipline and an entirely different understanding of costs versus benefits.

The popular HGTV show, *Designed to Sell*, takes modest, disorganized houses and turns them into gems for the resale market using a budget of $2,000. The changes are often very superficial, the materials inexpensive and the labor donated. Essentially, the theme is–throw out the old and put in the new. Suddenly, you have three offers and each $15,000 above your original asking price. And they do it all in a week.

Sounds like magic, and to a certain extent it is, in that the real estate markets of the last year or so have been so competitive that you could put anything up for sale and get your price. Of course, no one should assume that this trend will continue forever.

Further, the houses on the show are simple, small and single level. At no time do the producers suggest any major problems. However, they have hit on a very important part of buyer psychology: do not assume that the buyer can appreciate your hidden gem. Buyers have little imagination and a limited desire to redo a house once purchased. You have to lead them to the Promised Land, show them how the house could and should look.

The biggest challenge is not to renovate too much and not to spend too much. It is also important to know what is and what is not going to produce an immediate return on your investment. In addition, you want to make changes that are free of defect, and reflect what you promised to the new owner.

The Facts

Your strategy could simply be to sell the house as is, without changing anything. Clean up the clutter, rearrange the rooms, depersonalize the mantel and put the place up for sale. One problem with this strategy is that buyers want more—in particular, they want to be sure that after they move in the house will not fall down on them. Buyers crave comfort and reassurance.

If buyers see that ordinary repairs and some improvements have been made, they will be confident that the entire house is in good working order, which might convince them to make a larger offer. Much of house selling is psychological: Does the house satisfy my living needs *and* do I also feel that I got a good deal on the purchase?

Where do you begin the process as a remodeler who wants to sell rather than stay? First, do not overspend and do not redesign the house in any major way. Unless the kitchen and baths are a complete wreck, do not gut them and put in all new. If large, expensive projects are required to bring the house up to a reasonable standard, you own a distressed property and should market it accordingly. Assuming that this is not the case, do not try to anticipate what the buyer will want—you will be wrong.

Remodeling to sell is all about perceptions. One of those perceptions is that a messy, cluttered house has not been kept up. There may be no basis for this perception, but it is there. All the buyer sees is a mess with no potential. So your first task has nothing to do with remodeling at all; it is to get rid of all the junk.

Before making any decisions, get the opinion of at least three knowledgeable and local real estate agents. Consider taking a test run with the house as is. If you have done a sufficient job in presenting the house, a 30-day contract with an agent may be worthwhile. Market conditions, the house's location, its style or size, your school district—almost anything could elicit an offer without your spending much money. (However, be prepared, after an inspection, to make some repairs or changes, or to lower the price to cover essential repairs.)

You can always take the house off the market for a month or two, make your improvements and repairs, and put it back on the market based on the feedback from the first listing. What this market test provides is the specifics—you have real, market data to support your remodeling and its costs.

Be objective. We all have a sentimental attachment to their home, and feel that we have done a good job with repairs, improvements and decorating schemes. As you walk through the house, you may not see problems. Others, especially if they are professionals, will see them. Try not to take their comments personally; they are offered to get you the best price with the least amount of remodeling pain.

You cannot ignore major defects and expect to get full price for the property. Nor can you, by law, ignore health issues such as radon, asbestos, mold, fire hazards or electrical defects. Almost every state requires full disclosure at the time of sale. You absolutely must solve these problems. No one, unless they are willing to offer a substantially below market price, will take a house that is not in reasonable repair.

Once the clutter is cleared, professionally repair cracks, and caulk and paint the inside and outside of the house. Then sand the floors, clean or replace windows, add insulation and improve the curb appeal of the house. None of these improvements is particularly expensive.

The Solutions

First, get as many opinions as possible from a variety of sources as to what is wrong with your house. This includes friends, family, neighbors and your professional team (there are people who make a living staging houses for potential buyers). Put aside your feelings about your house and respect others' points of view.

Once you have cleared the house, start on the furniture and the flow of the house. Put extra chairs and tables in the basement. Show people that the house has plenty of space, that you can move around and that they would have plenty of room for their furniture. Open the drapes or, better yet, replace them with simple sheers or blinds. Exposed windows and lots of light make the rooms seem larger and friendlier.

Paint, paint and paint some more. Consider using neutral colors, thus making the house appealing no matter the furniture or future décor. However, if the house already has pleasant and appealing color coordination, keep it as is. Simply refresh it so that it looks like the rooms were just renovated.

Nothing scares buyers more than water stains or the impression that there is a leak somewhere. Solve these problems once and for all. Do not try to fool people by making temporary repairs; if there is a problem not disclosed it will come back to haunt you in 6 months when you get a letter from the buyer's lawyer.

Remove wallpaper, especially if it has been up for a few years, has a bold or bright pattern or looks faded or dated. Do not paint or paper over existing wallpaper; you will make the problem worse. Never add new wallpaper. Once the wallpaper is removed, you will have to remove the old paste, resize the wall and paint.

Curb appeal is crucial. Clean and repair the porch, lights, front door, sidewalks, lawn, front fence and landscaping. Pull out old, overgrown evergreens and shrubs. A few hundred dollars from the nursery can go a long way to luring buyers into your home. Make the front of the house clean, inviting and conventional.

There is typically no need to remodel the kitchen or baths, knock out walls or add a fireplace in order to sell your home. Remember the paint principle: cabinets and walls can be updated for very little. If you decide to replace appliances, buy the basics. You can still offer stainless steel; just buy units without all the bells and whistles. The buyer can upgrade them later.

The Resources

If you have cable, watch a few episodes of HGTV's *Design to Sell*. While you should not be taken in by the simplicity of it all, the principles behind the show are nonetheless excellent.

When you have finished your remodeling, visit *www.housevalues.com* and fill out the free questionnaire to get an idea of what your house is now worth. As with many sites, expect to be bombarded with advertisements for related services.

41

Remodeling Lite

The Challenge

Several months ago, a homeowner in the Northeast decided to sell. The large, turn-of-the-century home was too big and expensive–and considerable equity had built up over 20 years. With prospects of a near million-dollar asking price, an experienced real estate agent was invited to set a price and discuss what needed to be done to get top dollar.

The house was in excellent repair and the majority of the house was very appealing to buyers. However, the agent felt that a number of the rooms seemed dated. He suggested that the owners remodel portions of the home. The owners decided to take on some of the changes–some they did themselves, but most were hired out to competent contractors.

Three of four bathrooms were partially remodeled, including new tile and fixtures in the master and the first-floor half bath. New windows were installed where needed, the entire house was painted and new furniture was selectively added. In addition, there were changes in light fixtures, the basement was cleaned, new carpeting was laid in the master bedroom and additional storage was created in the master bathroom. The result–at the second meeting with the real estate agent, the suggested asking price moved well over $1 million.

By any standard for a twelve-room house, this remodeling could only be described as *lite*. (It is important to remember that most of the house had been continually updated, eliminating the need for huge changes.) The remodeling was so successful that the owners decided to stay in the house.

The lesson of this story and the challenge that it presents are much the same: Just how much do you really need and how much do you really want to spend? Sometimes it is the simple things that matter most. Before you charge ahead and spend a fortune, living in dust and clutter for weeks or months, take time to evaluate your situation and your needs.

The Facts

If you hate your house, a change of floor covering will not make you love it. If the kitchen is too small or the cabinets are in disrepair, painting the room will add nothing. If the arrangement or flow of the rooms is awkward or if there is not enough space, there is no lite solution. If you have to share a bathroom with five people, it gets old quickly.

On the other hand, assuming most issues with your house are not extreme, some smaller, specific and affordable changes might make all the difference. The assumption here is that you are trying your best to avoid an extreme makeover and can live with some compromises.

Start with a whole-house evaluation or inventory:

- Are there any structural issues, such as the foundation, slab, porches or decks, sagging floors or badly pitched roofs?
- What is the condition of the major house systems such as heating, air conditioning, electrical and plumbing?
- Does the roof need replacing?
- Evaluate the look, quality and function of the doors and windows; do they work and do they keep out the cold?
- What is the condition of the outside siding, stucco or brick?
- Are there sufficient bedrooms?
- What is the condition and size of the bathrooms?
- Review the kitchen and family room, assuming that they are probably the most important.
- What is the condition of the flooring in various rooms?
- Are you satisfied with the attic and basement, assuming that they are living spaces and not just storage?
- Do you have sufficient parking and what is the condition of the garage?
- Is there sufficient storage space?

These are all subjective questions. Ask other family members—particularly your spouse or partner—what they think about the house. Find out if there is general satisfaction with the house and the lifestyle that it affords.

If the house gets a passing grade of 80 percent or better, go through it with a different perspective. Ask yourselves what you do not like about the place, assuming that its bones are basically good and that you and your family function well in it. At this stage, do not factor in the cost or the resale value of any remodeling or changes that you might think need to be done.

Walk from room to room, make observations, take notes. Take your time. Move the furniture and look at the condition of everything, including the décor and furnishings. The kitchen and baths are probably the most important and also the most expensive spaces to change. Your primary task is to try to figure out what you can keep, not what should be taken out and replaced.

Remodeling lite takes into consideration a number of important issues:

- This is a starter house and you cannot afford to remodel extensively.
- You may be planning to move in 1 or 2 years.
- The neighborhood does not justify extensive remodeling.
- You simply do not have the time or interest to gut/rehab of your home.
- Your priorities are not in your home, but rather your family or career.
- Your spouse and family do not want to remodel the house.
- If you simplify the remodeling, you can do most of the work yourself.

The Solutions

Hire a decorator or a designer to walk through the house after you have done your evaluation. Bring along your list of problem areas. When you and the designer have finished your tour, attempt your first pass at a list of priorities. Your goal is not to remodel the entire house, but to make relatively inexpensive changes in order to build satisfaction and quality of lifestyle.

Focus your attention, time and money on one room at a time. Assuming you are starting with the kitchen, what changes can you make over 6 months that will materially affect the quality and functionality of the kitchen?

- Change the color of the cabinets by refinishing or repainting them.
- Resurface or replace (in kind and size) cabinet fronts and boxes.
- Replace the handles and door pulls.
- Are there small walls or islands that make the room look crowded and which could be removed?
- Do you need to add an island for more counter space and seating?
- If the appliances work, can you change their front panels to make them more contemporary?
- See if there are reasonable alternative to hard surfaces such as the floor, countertops and backsplash (splurge on one–marble on the counter tops–and save on the flooring).
- Paint, paint and paint again.

Apply the same process to each room. Assess each one slowly and systematically, changing only what absolutely needs to change. Ensure that the colors and flooring move from room to room with consistency and grace; you do not want harsh changes.

When in doubt about something, get rid of it. Take down complicated window treatments and replace with classic looks in drapes, blinds and shutters. Consider built-in furniture and cabinets, often available as semi-custom systems, to open the space and remove clutter.

Make every effort to add light, natural or otherwise, to enhance the feel and comfort of your rooms. If you cannot or do not want to enlarge the windows, add track lighting. Wash the walls with lights from inexpensive floor spots. Brighten wall colors, furniture patterns and flooring choices. When was the last time you changed fixtures in your rooms–things like ceiling lights and fans? Fans, for example, have come down in price dramatically, are easy to install and come in dozens of styles.

Consider removing interior doors that clutter the space. If you must have a door, use French doors or folding doors to maintain privacy but keep spaces open. Removing part of a wall, say in the kitchen, will open the space and allow for stools and a counter on the family or dining room side of the half wall. Instead of using walls to define space, use portable screens and furniture instead. They are flexible and can be removed at any time.

The Resources

Visit *www.tradebit.com* to find an advertisement for a book–actually a download– called *Home Remodeling Secrets: How to Create a Beautiful Home on a Shoestring Budget* (self published). This e-book is guaranteed by the author and covers all the basic concepts for remodeling and improving your home without spending a fortune.

An interesting and informative site is *www.onthehouse.com* with the Carey Brothers. Click on the tab called Tip of the Day and you will get free access to dozens of topics about home remodeling and improvement, many of them designed to assist you in your lite remodeling.

Feng Shui
Your Space

The Challenge

Feng shui is the ancient Chinese art of manipulating and arranging your surroundings through the placement of color and objects to attract positive life energy, or Chi (pronounced *chee*), so that it flows smoothly. When the energy around you is flowing freely, life is easier. If you experience setbacks and do not know why, maybe that energy is not flowing freely and everything is actually working against you.

The Chinese words *feng* and *shui* mean *wind* and *water*, symbolizing the importance of nature's role in our lives. The practice of feng shui can add ease, success and balance to your life.

Feng shui aims to balance Yin and Yang (two opposite forces in the universe which together form a balanced whole) in the flow of Chi using the basic five elements: earth, metal, water, wood and fire. Whether you are selecting a lot for your new home, remodeling, selling or just re-arranging your desk, there is a feng shui way.

The Facts

The five elements of feng shui influence our lives and our energy levels. Ensure that all elements are in balance. If one element is missing, it can be added; if one is too strong, another may be added to achieve balance.

Feng shui strategically places objects within a space to bring harmony to the environment. It can be as simple as placing a conversational grouping in the best location in your living room, or as complex as positioning your home in the best location on your property.

The Solutions

When building or remodeling your home, position rooms based on your daily routine. As a rule, rooms used primarily in the morning should face the east or south to maximize sunlight. Rooms occupied primarily after 2 p.m. should face south or west. A room facing west creates a comfortable gathering space. Rooms facing north are best used for activities that require concentration. Consider theses directions for the following rooms:

Direction	Rooms
East	Breakfast room
Southeast	Porch, computer space
Northeast	Bedroom
West	Evening gathering room
Southwest	Kitchen, dining room
Northwest	Library, playroom
North	Bathroom, storage, art or hobby space
South	Kitchen, gathering room, children's bedroom

To follow feng shui guidelines, identify the center of the building, as well as each area within it. Begin by overlaying a Bagua (pronounced *bog wa*) map over your living or working space. The map is divided into nine segments called *guas* that suggest the best areas for certain activities, furniture, decorative items and architectural features. The Bagua represents the eight building blocks of life: career, wisdom & knowledge, family & health, wealth, reputation & fame, love & marriage, children & creation and helpful people, plus the center area of Chi. Superimpose a Bagua map on specific spaces to obtain a reading of your current life, luck and future destiny. Problem areas may be balanced with celestial cures or lucky objects to eliminate negative energy and create positive energy. The nine Bagua areas include:

Area	Color	Description	Location*
Career	Black, blue & brown	Your job and the passage of life. Black also represents mood and perception.	North
Wisdom & Knowledge	Black, blue & green	This area represents learning, knowledge or study.	Northeast
Family & Health	Blue & green	Green represents physical and emotional health, your ancestors, current family, friends and co-workers and potential.	East
Wealth	Green, red & purple	Money and everything else that makes you feel wealthy or blessed. Purple represents spiritual guidance.	Southeast
Reputation & Fame	Red	Attraction, warmth and strength. This area represents how the world sees you.	South
Love & Marriage	Red, pink & white	Pink represents love and personal relationships through marriage, business partners or good friends.	Southwest
Children & Creation	White, yellow & pastels	Children, life, energy, current projects or anything creative.	West
Helpful People	Black, white & gray	Relationships with individuals outside your immediate family and friends. May include strangers, mentors or spiritual leaders.	Northwest
Center of Chi	Yellow & earth tones	Health and longevity. The center of the Bagua.	Central: harmonizes all areas

* Whole House. All positions start from the main door of a room or main entry to a house. Single room based on a north facing wall with a centered door entry.

Color	Association	Decorating materials
Red	Fire	**Fabrics/Materials:** silk, synthetics **Shapes/Textures/Patterns:** geometric or triangular shapes, animal designs and patterns **Art/Sculpture:** sunrises, sunflowers, geometric abstracts Artwork with red as the predominant color A wool area rug **Conveys:** Attention, passion, and take-charge, action
Green/aquas	Wood	**Fabrics:** cotton, rayon, linen **Shapes/Textures/Patterns:** Rectangles, stripes and leaf, flower, organic designs, columnar **Art/Sculpture:** pictures of trees, forest, flowers Add some wood for creativity Floral fabrics or wall covering Furniture with wood details A wooden baseboard, wainscot, or molding Fresh flowers and plants **Conveys:** Durable, supporting, enterprising and willingness to change
Blue/black	Water	**Fabrics:** see-thru and shimmering fabrics **Materials:** glass, mirrors, water features **Shapes/Textures/Patterns:** irregular and wavy shapes, paisley, tie-dye **Art/Sculpture:** depiction of any body of water Add some water for mind focus and sensitivity Crystal accessories and vase with fresh flowers An indoor running water sculpture Sconces with glass shades A painting of the ocean **Conveys:** Cooling, pacifying, all inclusive, imaginative
Yellow, terra cottas, earth tones and browns	Earth	**Material:** stone (jewelry), ceramics Shapes/Textures/Patterns: squares, checked patterns, bulky and flat-topped furniture or accessories **Art/Sculpture:** desert and landscapes Add earth for stability Terracotta planters Natural stepping stone entry Ceramic accessories **Conveys:** Secure, safe, constant, and dependable
White, silver, gold, copper, jewel tones	Metal	**Materials:** metal (jewelry) **Shapes/Textures/Patterns:** polka dots, semi-circles, dome-shaped, round **Art/Sculpture:** metal sculpture that has a feeling of abundance and expansion Add metal for financial growth Bronze door knobs A piece of sculpture A metal picture frame **Conveys:** Positive, innovative, whimsical, and adventurous

Determine the Bagua of the home by the location of the front door. Apply your map with the Wisdom & Knowledge and Career & Helpful People areas placed along the wall that contains your front door. The other areas will follow from there.

Here is a step-by-step guide to applying the Bagua map to your home, room, office or property:

Step 1: Draw a sketch of the home you wish to feng shui. Finish off any missing areas to form a square or rectangle.

Step 2: Divide your floor plan into nine equal squares. Your front door or entrance must be on the baseline on the Bagua map.

Step 3: From the front entrance fill in all areas of your home with the areas represented by the Bagua—career, family, wisdom, etc.

Step 4: Your diagram shows how all rooms in your home relate to the various guas. Compare how your room location relates to the Bagua map. If you have two+ floors, the areas and rooms on each story correspond to each other.

If you live in an L-shaped or U-shaped home, fill in any missing area with dotted lines to create a complete square. The same rules that apply to the house and interior rooms apply to the entire property. If you face your property from the street, the wealth area is the far left corner, while the career area is at the front and center of your property.

Review individual Bagua areas and include feng shui elements to enhance or balance the energy of the space. Example–in the wealth area of the room or home, place a bowl filled with coins to represent prosperity. In the love & marriage room, place your wedding picture in a red, white or pink frame, two vases with pink flowers, a book of love poems, or anything that represents romance.

A positive feng shui environment is best achieved gradually. Set goals to enhance one or two areas of your home or room at a time, then expand the practice to each room in the house to create a positive energy flow.

Colors also create a positive energy. For example, wealth area colors are represented with green and purple. Consider painting your rear left room a vibrant shade of green. If that room is a bedroom, you might want to use a deep rich purple bedspread or comforter. If your kitchen is in the center of your house, or in the Chi area, paint it a vibrant, sunny yellow and accessorize with muted earth tones. You are limited only by your imagination.

The Resources

Additional online resources to provide feng shui advice and assistance.

www.webterrace.com/fengshui/. This Website will help you understand the origins of feng shui and how you can improve your living environment through its simple rules and practices.

www.fengshuihelp.com. Provides free advice to people who want to achieve balance and harmony in their lives.

Saving Energy
Is the Key

The Challenge

For homeowners these days, energy savings are a huge issue. Global competition for oil and gas, a lack of investment in petroleum industry infrastructure over the last 20 years, environmental concerns about new coal-fired or atomic energy electricity-generating plants–these have all set the stage for an ongoing energy shortage in the United States and the rest of the world.

Besides energy costs, the environment–in particular, global warming–is also a major issue. No matter your motivation, however, you should think about energy use and conservation when remodeling any part of the home,

The older your home, the more important the issue of energy savings. Insulation, plastic wrapping, caulking, energy efficient windows and vapor barriers in the interior were not used a generation ago, simply because heating oil and natural gas were very inexpensive.

Your challenge is to introduce as many energy-saving features into your remodeling. If you plan to work systematically throughout the house over a number of years, you cannot implement an energy savings program all at one time, but you can do a very good job as you attach and remodel each room.

The Facts

Your appliances and home electronics are responsible for about 20 percent of your energy bills. By shopping for appliances with the ENERGY STAR label and turning off appliances when they are not in use, you can achieve real savings in your monthly energy bill.

Heating and cooling account for about 56 percent of the energy use in a home. Various technologies are available for heating and cooling your home. They offer a wide range of efficiencies in converting their energy sources into useful heat or cool air.

You can reduce your home's heating and cooling costs by as much as 30 percent through proper insulation and air-sealing techniques. These techniques will also make your home more comfortable. Conduct a home energy audit to assess where your home may be losing energy through air leaks or inadequate insulation

Water heating can account for 14 percent to 25 percent of household energy. You can reduce your monthly water heating bills by selecting the appropriate water heater for your home or pool, and by using energy-efficient water-heating strategies.

Buying a bigger room air-conditioning unit will not necessarily make you feel more comfortable during heatwaves. In fact, a room air conditioner that is too big for a specific area will perform less efficiently and less effectively than a smaller, properly sized unit (room units that run for relatively long periods of time work better than those that continually switch off and on).

Central air-conditioning systems need to be sized by professionals. If you have such a system, set the fan to shut off at the same time as the cooling unit (compressor– do not use the system's central fan to provide circulation; instead, use circulating fans in individual rooms.

The Solutions

When looking for ways to save energy in your home remodeling, try not only to improve your existing heating and cooling system, but also to consider the energy efficiency of the supporting equipment and the possibility of either adding supplementary sources of heating or cooling, or simply replacing your system altogether.

- Use fans during the summer to create a wind chill effect that will make your home more comfortable.
- Turn off kitchen, bath and other ventilating fans 20 minutes after you are done cooking or bathing to retain heated air.
- Install a programmable thermostat that can adjust the temperature according to your schedule.
- Insulate your hot water heater and hot water pipes.
- Insulate heating ducts in unheated areas such as attics and crawlspaces, and keep them in good repair to prevent heat loss of up to 60 percent.
- Consider overhauling–or even replacing–your furnace or heat pump.
- Conduct an energy audit of your home to find air leaks and to check for the proper level of insulation. Common sources of air leaks include cracks around windows and doors, gaps along baseboard, mail chutes, cracks in brick, siding, stucco or foundation, or where any external lines enter the home.

- To test for air leaks on your own, hold a lit candle next to windows, doors, electrical outlets or light fixtures on a windy day.
- Tape clear plastic sheeting to the inside of your window frames if drafts, water condensation, or frost are present.
- Plug air leaks with caulking, sealing or weather stripping to save 10 percent or more on your energy bill.
- Adequate insulation in your attic, ceilings, exterior and basement walls, floors and crawlspaces–as recommended for your geographical area–can reduce energy bills by up 30 percent.
- ENERGY STAR windows can reduce heat loss from air leakage, and reflect heat back into the room during the winter months.
- In cold climates, ENERGY STAR windows can reduce your heating bills by 40 percent compared to uncoated, single-pane windows.
- Close fireplace dampers when not in use. Warm air escapes up chimneys.
- Install task lighting–such as under-counter kitchen lights or bathroom mirror lights–to reduce the need for ambient lighting of large spaces.
- Use dimmers, motion sensors or occupancy sensors to automatically turn on or off lighting as needed.
- Install fluorescent light fixtures for all ceiling- and wall-mounted fixtures that will be on for more than 2 hours each day.
- Use ENERGY STAR labeled lighting fixtures.
- Consider light wall colors to minimize the need for artificial lighting.
- Use compact fluorescent light bulbs (CFLs) in place of incandescent bulbs to save about 50 percent on your lighting costs. CFLs use only one-fourth the energy and last up to 10 times longer.
- Turn your lights off when you leave a room. Standard incandescent light bulbs should be turned off when not needed. Fluorescent lights should be turned off whenever you will be away for 15 minutes or more.
- During winter, open curtains on your south-facing windows during the day to allow sunlight to naturally heat your home. Close them at night to reduce the chill you may feel from cold windows.
- Installing a skylight can provide your home with daylight and warmth. It can also help minimize your heating, cooling and lighting costs.

You have many options for using renewable energy at home–from solar-powered outdoor lights to buying renewable energy from your utility. You can even produce solar electricity at home with photovoltaic (PV) cells.

- A new home provides the best opportunity for designing and orienting the home to take advantage of the sun's rays. A well-oriented home admits low-angle winter sun to reduce heating bills and rejects overhead summer sun to reduce cooling bills.

- Many consumers buy electricity made from renewable energy sources like the sun, wind, water, plants and earth's internal heat. This is one of the easiest ways to use renewable energy without having to invest in equipment or take on extra maintenance.
- If you have a swimming pool or hot tub, you can use solar power to cut pool-heating costs. Most solar pool heating systems are cost-competitive with conventional systems. This is actually the most cost-effective use of solar energy.
- If you have made your home as energy-efficient as possible, and you have very high electricity bills and a good solar resource, consider generating your own electricity using PV cells. New products are available that integrate PV cells with the roof, making them much less visible than older systems.

If the following conditions apply, you might want to do more research to see if investing in PV is right for you:

- Your site has adequate solar resources.
- A grid connection is not available in your area or can be made only through an expensive power line extension.
- You want to gain energy independence from your power provider.
- You are willing to pay more up front to reduce the environmental impact of your electricity use.
- Your power provider will connect your system to the electricity grid and buy any excess power you produce.

The Resources

Replacing appliances during renovation not only makes the house look up-to-date, but also saves energy in the long run and reduces operating costs substantially. Find retailers near you at *www.energystar.gov* when you are ready to replace your heating and cooling systems, as well as your appliances, lighting, windows, office equipment and home electronics.

To find out if your state, city or utility offers rebates, tax credits or other incentives for renewable sources of energy, visit *www.dsireusa.org*. These kinds of financial incentives may influence your decision to use conventional or other energy sources.

Remodeling You Can Live With As You Age

The Challenge

There are homeowners who remodel with the idea that this will be the last home they will ever own–because they are so committed to the community, like the house so much or are at an age where the thought of moving in a few years is just not realistic. No matter your situation, you might give some consideration to making changes that will allow you more flexibility in the future and make the house user-friendly as you age.

When you are in your 30s or 40s, it is difficult to imagine getting older or infirm, but be assured that anticipating the need to adapt the home to your changing health (or that of parents or other relatives who might come to live with you) is good planning. Many changes that will make the house more adaptable do not cost a great deal–for example, widening doorways to 40 inches in order to accommodate a wheelchair. If you are changing a doorway anyway, why not make it bigger?

The challenge is to make changes that anticipate your needs and still keep your home attractive should you decide to sell. You limit your customer base severely if the house looks as though it was designed only for senior citizens. On the other hand, many of the features that help older homeowners are also good safety practice–grab bars in the shower stall, for example.

Not all remodeling that anticipates the owners' getting older relate to health and safety issues. You may plan for fewer bedrooms once your children go to college and then move out on their own–rumor has it that some of them actually do move out! Some changes may be made so that spaces can be used for other purposes–a home business after you retire, hobbies or other personal interests. The key is to ensure as much adaptability as possible.

The Facts

There are an estimated 76 million baby boomers in the United States. Many do not wish to move out of their homes or neighborhoods. Instead they are embracing a design and remodeling trend called aging-in-place. Part of this trend is the use of so-called universal design, which came into common use in the 1990s with the passage of the Americans with Disabilities Act, which required public spaces to be more accessible.

The first efforts at universal design were ugly and institutional, and were not readily adapted for home use—nor were they appreciated or valued. But improvements in design and function are talking place all the time. Consider some of these changes and products:

- Motion-detector faucets.
- Handhold recesses in the shower rather than grab bars.
- Sinks that can be raised or lowered.
- Levers or paddles rather than doorknobs.
- Lower shelves and light switches—the differences can be very subtle.
- Touch dimmer switches.
- New designs in washers and dryers.
- Tiled seat in the shower rather than institutional stainless steel.
- Lower oven heights.
- Use of Lazy Susans to make cabinets more accessible.
- Wider doorways.

The most important part of making such changes is to keep them unobtrusive

The total market for remodeling amounts to about $214 billion annually. The aging-in-place portion of this amount is currently small, though estimates suggest that within 10 years it could rise to $20-25 billion a year. The Remodelers Council, in association with the American Association of Retired People, has developed a training program called Certified Aging-in-Place Specialists (CAPS) for remodelers who wish to specialize in this kind of construction.

There is an interesting conflict in some circles between those who want to make housing more accessible and purists in historical districts who fight vigorously against changes that are not in character with the original neighborhood. This difference of opinion is just starting to affect trends that support aging-in-place renovation.

The Solutions

The key to unobtrusive, universal design is to envision what you might use the space for in the future. In other words, do not build in expensive obstacles that might entail a totally new renovation 10 years from now because you are older and less able to manage stairs or a bathroom.

Focus on possible future first-floor living. For example, a large family room can be remodeled with the idea that all or part of the space will eventually become a downstairs bedroom. If you are remodeling a first floor bathroom off the family room, make it a bit larger, with doors that are more accessible, and include safety features.

Vary the heights of countertops, knowing that most of them will be used when standing up. Add a lower countertop, perhaps at the height of a typical table, under which a chair (or chairs) could easily be placed for food preparation. The different counter heights can add charm and interest to the room, especially if you vary the countertop surfaces to make the lower level surface look like built-in furniture.

If your plans call for rebuilding a staircase, this is the perfect opportunity to renovate with the future in mind. Stairs are the single greatest obstacle to aging-in-place (remember, they can also be difficult and dangerous for children as well). Widen the stairs, lover the risers and add more landing spots on the stairs. Make your staircase grand—an invitation to see the rest of the house and accessible to people of all ages.

Many new homes are adding elevators or lifts—a great idea if you can afford it and can incorporate the fixture in an existing building. The good news is that demand for mobility between floors is growing, and companies are responding with new, increasingly affordable products. Otis Elevator Co. reports that sales for home elevators have increased 12 percent to 15 percent per year for the last 3 years. In addition to functionality, there is a growing opinion that elevators add value to a house at the time of sale. Pneumatic lifts are cheaper and easier to install in existing housing.

While major renovation may allow for significant changes at the time of construction, there are many, smaller ways to improve the livability of your home without making it look institutional or awkward:

- A greater number and variety of lights, each controlled by its own dimmer switch.
- Improved access to garages and parking spaces.
- At least one doorway without steps.
- Electrical outlets 18 inches from the floor, rather than the standard 12 inches.
- Light switches at 42 inches.

- Strobe light smoke detectors (as well as the shrill sound).
- Non-skid flooring.
- Lower faucets in the shower.
- More space between fixtures and cabinets in kitchens and bathrooms.
- Pull-out shelves in cabinets.
- Side-by-side refrigerator.
- Built-in seating at least 18 inches off the floor.
- Raised toilets.
- Raised garden beds.
- Front-end loading washer and dryer.
- Full-length sidelights so that anyone of any size can see who is at the door.
- Package shelf or bench on the front porch.
- A covered porch.
- Larger thermostats, slightly lowered.

An important issue as you get older is the outside set of stairs that provides access to the house. If you are remodeling a kitchen, family room or some other first-floor space, this might be the ideal time to find a place to have easy access to the house. A patio door without a threshold and limited (or no) stairs would be ideal. Instead of stairs, you could introduce an interesting feature, such as a graduated ramp that is designed as part of the landscape.

Many of the items suggested for making your home friendlier as you grow older can add to your renovation budget, you may not be able to afford them all at one time. Naturally, it is important to make those changes that require significant work while the room or rooms are open and under construction. You can always add more lighting or lower the height of the thermostat without significant cost. Decide what is essential and go from there.

The Resources

An elevator can be a wonderful accessory or an absolute necessity. In either case, visit *www.daytonaelevator.com* to get an excellent idea about the available options.

Aging-in-Place (Hawthorn Press, 2002) is a fine book that covers many of the topics discussed in this chapter. It is available at *www.amazon.com*.

Children and Remodeling Fun

The Challenge

As a general rule, kids and household renovation do not mix. Whether living in or moving out during construction (see Chapter 23: *Should You Live In or Move Out During Construction?*), children of all ages will react differently than expected. Like adults, they are challenged by change. What is wrong with our current home?, they ask. And yes, they want a new family room, but without any mess, any effort or any break in their normal routine.

It is hard to communicate to smaller children what is going on. They will not understand that the renovation will allow them to have their own bath, for example, or not have to share a bedroom with a sibling. Younger children like stable routines and a major home renovation is anything but stable or routine. It is disruptive and can be threatening.

Middle school children and teenagers can appreciate the benefits of renovation and may be very excited about it. They will want to understand the renovation pretty much in terms of how it will benefit them. The prospects of a basement room, fully equipped and remodeled, where they can spend time with their friends is uppermost in their minds. Relieving crowding in bedrooms and bathrooms is also a huge attraction.

It is possible that a child may not like the fact that their familiar environment is going to change dramatically. Why is her bedroom off limits and why does she have to share a bedroom with her sister? Strangers constantly in and out of the house can cause fear or anxiety. Do not be surprised if children respond badly to the smells of paint or the loud noises generated by renovation. You will not like a lot of the disruption, so why expect them to manage without complaining?

The challenge, then, is to get all the kids involved, secure and happy, and to make the renovation not too hard on them—or on you, for that matter!

The Facts

No matter the age of your children, goodwill will improve greatly if the renovation becomes a family project—though be warned that college-age children may assume, rightly or wrongly, that you are trying to get rid of them. In any case, total family involvement will work better than just ignoring their feelings or concerns.

You need to do a little explaining, particularly about why the family will renovate the home and what the benefits will be. Once the plans are firm, set up a meeting and explain what is planned and how long it will take. Give as much information as you can, but include only relevant items—no child needs to sit through a discussion of sistering ceiling joists, for example.

Children do need to express themselves, so allow the opportunity on a regular basis—perhaps every night, if they are younger. The older children will not need a specific time to complain—they will do it morning, noon and night. But take the time to listen to some of their complaints before getting too frustrated.

A lot of tension will center on friends and everyday routines and activities. Work hard to keep the routine going and have friends over, even if it means more inconvenience. This may take a bit of creativity—for example, turning the dining room into a place to play video games—but it will be well worth it.

Children respond to pictures and physical objects rather than verbal descriptions. If you are building an extension to the house, walk outside and show them where the addition will be.

Involving the children does not necessarily mean that you bow to their every whim, but there are simple compromises. They should have a say about the new color of their rooms and the kind of carpeting. Special features such as colorful blinds and sports-related décor can go a long way.

The Solutions

For younger children, try to make a game or adventure out of renovation. Use some of the old magazine clippings you have been saving and share some of the ideas you have been considering. Draw a picture of your house and fill in the rooms with different pictures and clippings, coloring the rooms as they are completed. Perhaps you could have special treats at particular milestones.

Do everything you can to create and build excitement (without going overboard) before, during and after construction. If you are enthusiastic and excited, it will be contagious. When difficult times come around, discuss them only with your spouse and the contractor.

Try not to pin down an exact date when the work will be completed. Rather, give a date farther in the future than what you expect; if a certain date is set in everyone's mind, all sorts of frustration will arise if there are delays.

If you are not living at the site, visit it regularly so that the kids can see what is going on. Make the visits weekly, or whenever you can show off substantial progress. Walking through the new family room or climbing the temporary stairs to see the new bedrooms can be great fun and a morale booster. If your house looks the same from 1 week to the next, postpone the visit–seeing that nothing has been done will do more harm than good.

Inform your contractor of these visits, so that the site is clean and safe. To avoid getting in the way during construction, make your visits on Sundays, knowing that work is halted for the day and the family can talk freely about the renovation. As you look around, train the older kids to look carefully at the work–young eyes can spot things that you may miss.

Show architectural or designer drawings to the children, especially the older ones. Make them a lesson in basic math and geometry. If your math skills are rusty, ask the contractor or an assistant to go over the diagrams with the kids. Have everyone replicate the measurements that are on the plans and draw their own version. Then walk the physical space with them so that they can transfer diagrams to reality.

Almost all manufacturers and suppliers have Websites in color displaying their products and materials–your kitchen appliances, the color of the siding, the look of the new windows, even the paint in the new bedrooms. Show the children how color is used and the various combinations that designers and homeowners use (see The Resources at the end of chapter).

Use design software to recreate the look and feel of the design. Show your children the builder's plans in three dimensions using CAD-CAM software. If you do not want to buy design software, your designer or architect will do a demo on their laptop.

If you are doing the work yourself or are the general contractor, get your grade school and high school children to help. Older kids especially can tote that barge and lift that bail. Put their youth and strength to work–let them help to keep the site clean, drive to pick up materials, assist with demolition. Common sense should dictate what they can and cannot do. Ensure their absolute safety with the proper eyewear, shoes and gloves.

If you are staying in the house, there will be times when everyone will need to get away for a day or two (or more). It may be a good idea to let your children have a friend or two along so that they can make up for lost opportunities to share time and interests.

One of the worst-case scenarios is when a project goes well beyond its completion day. Plan for this eventuality. Carefully explain that the renovation is going to take longer, and avoid a second, firm completion date. If you sense that the renovation is slowing down or will face certain problems, begin communicating this to the children. Breaking the bad news in bits and pieces might lessen the impact and allow children to get used to the idea that construction will continue for a time longer.

When the renovation is completed, have a family celebration–perhaps on the day you are putting furniture and belongings in their new home.

The Resources

Color and color combinations can be fascinating to adults and children. HGTV has a regular show devoted to the use of color, called *Get Color!* Watch it as a family and then go to *www.hgtv.com*; part of the site shows how to use color in various combinations.

There are many relatively inexpensive home design software packages that can be used to involve the children. Consider *Better Homes and Gardens Interior Designer, Floor Plan Design Suite Version 9* or *Broderbund 3D Home Architect Home Design Deluxe 6*. All are available at *www.amazon.com*.

Handling Stress
During Remodeling

The Challenge

People have different stress levels. Some have a remarkable ability to go with the flow, and not get worked up about problems. Others–perhaps the majority of homeowners during construction and renovation–fall in the other camp. The changes to the normal household routine, the decisions that have to be made and the overall pace of activity can be overwhelming.

To manage stress, try to anticipate its potential causes and develop specific, stress-reducing strategies for everyone in the household. (It does not help if one spouse finds relief, while the other spouse and the kids are disorganized and out of sorts.)

According to the Holmes Stress Scale, changes in your residence or living conditions are one of the top 25 stress-inducing situations. To alleviate renovation-related stress, you should first plan and then carefully consider what you are about to take on: The costs, the time commitment, the disruption of the household routine and the need to manage the contractor and his workers.

Finally, there is one simple and universal truth about home remodeling: What can go wrong will go wrong, and something will go wrong at some point. Accept this.

The Facts

The first home renovation, major or minor, is always the hardest. That is why it is a good idea to start slowly, with smaller, more manageable projects, before you plunge into an attic renovation or build an addition. Take on the bathroom or replace the flooring in the bedrooms. Analyze and understand the process, your successes and failures, before moving on. A survey by a remodeling association reported that remodeling the kitchen was always the most stressful because living without a kitchen causes the most inconvenience.

There are many situations that you can control during renovation and there are a host of problems you cannot. Make a list of each category, try to separate them in your own mind and keep them handy when you react to the inevitable problems. For example, some of the matters you do have control over are:

- Your attitude.
- The budget.
- When you schedule work.
- Planning the entire project carefully.
- Preventing change orders.
- Accidents on the job site–up to a point.
- Tickets or fines from the city or village.
- Whining or difficult children.
- Spouses who will not help.
- Underestimating costs.
- Not enough money to complete the work.
- Believing you can do the work yourself (and you cannot).
- Not asking for help from friends or family.

And here are a few things that you cannot control and should not feel frustrated about:

- There will be delays, downtime and missed schedules.
- Materials will be the wrong size, the wrong color or just plain wrong.
- Materials will show up late.
- There will be complaints from the neighbors.
- You have too much on your plate with work, kids and social responsibilities.
- There are going to be problems with the contractor over schedules, cleanliness of the work site, costs, quality or all of the above.
- There will be unexpected surprises, such as defective flooring, foundations or wiring–that is why you have a contingency in your budget and in your schedule.

Money is one of the most frequently argued about subjects between partners. Financial planning for your renovation–and money management once it begins– will go a long way to preventing stress. The more time you spend on planning, the less chance that the issue of money will drag you down.

Money is not the only thing that can disrupt harmony between partners. Disagreement about what will or will not be included in the renovation, as well as about the style of the renovation, can also cause friction. Because you are married, it does not mean that you have the same desires and tastes.

Identify in yourself and your partner some of the typical symptoms of stress:

For example, anxiety, depression, inability to concentrate, lack of patience, irritability over small matters, chronic fatigue, self-criticism, quickness to anger, sleeplessness, headaches or stomachaches, drinking more than usual, and unusual eating habits.

The Solutions

Be realistic about what you can and cannot take on at any one time. If your plans are grand but your patience and budget are not, break the work down to more manageable schedules and payment plans. Write up a long-term plan with both your architect and contractor present. Staging work allows you and your family to take a break, thus reducing stress.

Hiring the right contractor can greatly reduce stress. If your contractor is skilled and manages problems calmly and professionally, he or she is an invaluable asset.

Talk to friends, family and neighbors who have gone through an extensive renovation and learn from their experiences. Try to find out what the hot buttons were during construction—everyone has something that really makes them angry and upset.

Make a checklist of situations that might happen. Anticipate what you might do if, for example:

- The contractor quits.
- The budget is 30 percent higher than planned.
- The colors or design are wrong.
- There are hidden problems that were unknown at the time the job was bid.

The list goes on and on. Visualize your reaction and plan your solutions. Or at least try to ask your friends and family what they would or did do in similar circumstances. Have a back-up plan.

Perspective is everything. If you anticipate that problems will happen, you can minimize their effects. Even during a so-called crisis, stay focused on the ultimate goal: a beautiful new kitchen or family room or addition—or whatever your plans call for. See yourself and your family using and enjoying the new rooms.

Flexibility can be a lifesaver. Let us say you want a Sub-Zero in the new kitchen. When it comes time to put it in, it will not fit. You can rant and rave, or you can be flexible and decide that an alternative will work. Just how important are one or two items in the larger scheme of renovation? Is it worth putting yourself through the frustration?

Moving out during construction, or simply avoiding the work area, will help everyone's nerves. Hovering over workman just slows down progress. Shouting about problems does nothing–contractors will just ignore you or quit the scene.

Plan activities that you and the family enjoy. This will give you a break from a chaotic schedule. Take time to relax, visit friends, go to the city, take a weekend trip–do something you enjoy to compensate for the additional pressure.

If you are in conflict–for example, with the contractor–get one person to do the negotiations and have a face-to-face over the issues at hand. Ganging up on the contractor will only harm your efforts to complete the work. The best negotiator should take the lead. Be firm, concise and do not make your discussions personal. This is a business discussion and saying things you later regret will only increase your stress levels–and decrease your chances of getting help and advice in the future.

Two-o'clock-in-the-morning anxiety is always the worst–everything is exaggerated and nothing can be done to resolve the anxiety. Keep a pad and pencil at your bedside. Keep them with you throughout the day. Write down issues, concerns and problems–of course, solutions are welcome as well. Talk openly to your spouse about problems. Simply put–do not bottle up your concerns.

Physical activity is a great stress reducer. Walking, jogging, cleaning the house, chopping wood, cleaning up the work site–almost anything that brings a sweat will help you relieve the pressure and make you feel like you have control over your life (and your remodeling).

The Resources

Many online medical sites have valuable and useful information about stress and stress-related symptoms. Visit *www.webmd.com* and search under *stress*. You will find a series of useful and entertaining articles, all free of charge.

The Relaxation and Stress Reduction Handbook (New Harbinger Publications, 2000) is a useful and relatively inexpensive paperback that is highly rated with reviewers. Also consider *Less Stress* (Siloam Press, 2005); there is also an audio version. Visit *www.amazon.com* for more information on these and other books.

Taxes, the IRS and Your Basis When Selling Your Remodeled Home

The Challenge

This book repeatedly recommends proper record-keeping. At no other time are detailed records more important than when you decide to sell a home in which you have done substantial improvements.

Real estate prices are higher than ever and will likely increase at solid, steady rates. Your overall goal is to sell your home at as large a profit as possible and pay as little taxes as possible. This is best achieved if you understand the basics of tax law and policy, and if you have records to support your *basis* in your house.

The Facts

Use a tax preparer when you sell your improved home. Presumably, you will make a profit when you sell. The IRS has a number of rules and restrictions in this area. Recognizing that tax gains on houses can cost individuals a lot of money, allowances are made to protect some of those gains from ordinary taxes.

You may qualify to exclude from your income all or part of any gain from the sale of your main home (ordinarily the one you live in most of the time). To claim the exclusion, you must meet ownership and use tests. That is, during the 5-year period ending on the date of the sale, you must have:

- Owned the home for at least 2 years (the ownership test).
- Lived in the home as your main home for at least 2 years (the use test).

If you have a gain from the sale of your main home, you may be able to exclude up to $250,000 of the gain from your income ($500,000 on a joint return in most cases).

- If you can exclude all of the gain, you do not need to report the sale on your tax return.
- If you have a gain that cannot be excluded, it is taxable. Report it on *Schedule D (Form 1040)*.

Unfortunately, you cannot report a loss for income tax purposes on the sale of your main house. (If the house was converted to income property at sometime, that may be a different story). You do not have to report the sale of your main home on your tax return unless you have a gain and at least part of it is taxable.

You can exclude gain only from the sale of your main home. You must pay tax on the gain from selling any other home.

If you have done significant remodeling, the issue of basis is important. Basis is your starting point either for figuring a gain or loss if you later sell your home, or for figuring depreciation if you later use part of your home for business purposes or for rent. While you own your home, you may either add or subtract certain items (adustments) from your basis. The new basis is called your adjusted basis.

Understand these terms when you first acquire your home, because you must keep track of your basis and adjusted basis, and keep records of the events that affect them.

If you buy or build your home, your cost is your basis. If you receive your home as a gift, your basis is usually the same as the adjusted basis of the person who gave you the property. If you inherit your home, the fair market value at the date of the decedent's death is generally your basis.

The cost of your home (including any debt you assumed) includes the amount you paid for it plus most settlement or closing costs. If you built your home, your cost includes most closing costs paid when you bought the land or settled on your mortgage. (The basis of a cooperative apartment is the amount you paid for your shares in the corporation that owns or controls the property, including any purchase commissions or other costs of acquiring the shares.)

There may be times when real estate taxes become part of your basis. Seek advice if you are unsure about this. If you paid any part of the seller's share of the real estate taxes (the taxes up to the date of sale), and the seller did not reimburse you, add those taxes to your basis. If the seller paid any of your share of the real estate taxes (the taxes beginning with the date of sale), you can still deduct those taxes, but do not include them in your basis. If you did not reimburse the seller, you must reduce your basis by the amount of those taxes.

For most homeowners, the basis can rise and fall, so keep good records. Most improvements add to the basis of a home. Improvements are any changes that materially affect the value of your home, considerably prolong its useful life or adapt it to a new use.

When making improvements, the amount you add to your basis is the actual cost of remodeling, including costs for labor and materials (excluding your own labor). Any expenses related to an improvement can increase your basis.

Many homeowners fail to make the distinction between an improvement and a repair. A repair keeps your home in ordinary, efficient operating condition. It does not add value to your home per se.

Here are just a few examples of improvements that can increase your basis:

- Putting an addition on to the home.
- Replacing the entire roof.
- Paving your driveway.
- Installing central air conditioning.
- Rewiring your home.
- Adding a recreation room to the basement.
- Building a fence.

Other items are not so obvious, such as.

- Abstract fees (abstract of title fees).
- Charges for installing utility services.
- Legal fees for title search and preparation of the sales contract and deed.
- Rcording fees, surveys and transfer taxes.

The Solutions

Keep full, accurate records so that you can support the basis and adjusted basis of your home if you sell. You should have the orginal purchase contract and settlement papers, receipts, canceled checks or contracts for any improvements you have made to the house. Keep the records until you sell, gift or otherwise dispose of the home.

Use the following record keeper (next page) to track improvements in your home over the years. Remove any improvements that are no longer part of your main home. For example, if you put carpeting in your home and later replace it with new carpeting, remove the cost of the first carpeting.

(a) Type of Improvement	(b) Date	(c) Amount	(a) Type of Improvement	(b) Date	(c) Amount
Additions:			**Heating & air conditioning:**		
Bedroom			Heating system		
Bathroom			Central air conditioning		
Deck			Furnace		
Garage			Duct work		
Porch			Central humidifier		
Patio			Filtration system		
Storage shed			Other		
Fireplace					
Other			**Electrical:**		
			Lighting fixtures		
Lawn & Grounds:			Wiring upgrades		
Landscaping			Other		
Driveway					
Walkway			**Plumbing:**		
Fences			Water heater		
Retaining wall			Soft water system		
Sprinkler system			Filtration system		
Swimming pool			Other		
Exterior lighting					
Other			**Insulation:**		
			Attic		
Communications:			Walls		
Satellite dish			Floors		
Intercom			Pipes and duct work		
Security system			Other		
Other					
			Interior Improvements:		
Miscellaneous:			Built-in appliances		
Storm windows and doors			Kitchen modernization		
Roof			Bathroom modernization		
Central vacuum			Flooring		
Other			Wall-to-wall carpeting		
			Other		

The Resources

You can find much more on the subject of basis for homeowners who have made improvements and plan to sell their homes. See IRS *Publication 530* at *www.irs.gov*. To gain access to these and other forms throughout this book, visit *www.encouragementpress.com.* There is no registration required. All forms are free to our readers. You can include your e-mail address to learn more about other Encouragement Press books and products.

Putting On
the Ritz

The Challenge

Susan and Damien live in 1929 brick and stucco house in a comfortable, established area of Minneapolis. The house is a classic four over four, with a small bump-out on the first floor that includes a pantry, mudroom and enclosed stairs. The house has two stories, four bedrooms, a dining room, a living room and a small library/family room.

The house has a side driveway with a detached garage, which is not in the same style as the rest of the house. The lot is large and oddly shaped, with substantial front and back yards. Access to the back, however, is limited to the rather narrow driveway. With a shallow attic and a basement with low ceilings, the couple is faced with the task of finding space for a growing family.

There are restrictions placed by the township on what can be done to the front of the building. In any case, zoning laws will not allow for any kind of addition on the front or the sides of the house. The focus, not surprisingly, turns to the rear of the house and the separate garage.

House appreciation in this part of Minneapolis has been substantial–with this house, around 30 percent over the past 18 months. This is largely attributable to the quality of the local school district as well as the neighborhood's proximity to downtown Minneapolis.

Planning to refinance the house in order to make necessary repairs, Susan and Damien have hired an architect to assist them. One of the first problems is the fact that the house was built with brick–a color and style that is no longer available. Further, the bump-out does not have a substantial foundation. The garage, while sound and large enough for their needs, stands out from the rest of the house–it is covered in white aluminum siding.

The interior of the house has charm and warmth but lacks a bathroom, kitchen and living space to accommodate a growing family. Beamed ceilings, built-in cabinets around a wood-burning fireplace and cove molding make the rooms glow. Previous owners have taken good care of the plaster walls, leaded-glass windows and hardwood floors.

The goal is to add a two story-addition to the house without destroying its character or charm. Further, they need contemporary bathrooms and an interior style that will match and complement the original. None of this will be easy or cheap.

The Facts

The couple does not have to search far for a contractor. Susan's parents completed substantial work on their home 2 years earlier and had a great experience with the contractor/architect. His specialty is renovation of period houses. As a licensed architect, he is active in the restoration and preservation movements in the Minneapolis/St. Paul area, and has agreed to take on the project.

He insists on matching materials as nearly as possible. This means that the windows will be wood, not vinyl; the new flooring will be oak parquet; and drywall will be coated with plaster. The couple's needs and the contractor's insistence on certain levels of quality make it difficult to match the budget with reality.

In working with the couple, the architect assembled a basic plan for the renovation:

- Major emphasis on the creation of a larger kitchen, one in which improvements can be added at a later time.
- A first-floor family room, open to the kitchen with substantial built-in storage along the north wall.
- Installing a wood-burning stove in the family room instead of a much more expensive fireplace.
- Keeping the first-floor bath as-is to save some money, but using painted bead board instead of tile and replacing the existing fixtures with medium-grade products.
- Borrowing some space from the large living room to add a formal entry way, with a large down-stairs closet.
- Moving the basement stairs to a new location off the family room in order to eliminate doors in the kitchen and to allow for a walk-in pantry.
- Installing wood floors on the lower-level addition to match the existing house, including cove molding and window trim stained to match.
- Adding French doors for windows on the south side of the house, all of which open onto a simple wood deck (which can be expanded later).

- Retaining the existing garage, but removing the aluminum siding, adding a new period garage door and covering the garage with stucco to match the house.
- Demolition of the old bump-out, but recycling the bricks by incorporating them into the new addition to carry through the look and feel of the rest of the house.
- Creation of a master bedroom suite on the second level on top of the new family room/kitchen on the first floor.
- Designing a simple floor plan, which can be updated at a future time–consisting of carpeted floors, in-store fixtures and tile for the bathroom, and period pieces to complement the older portions of the house.
- Demolition of the existing master bedroom, using part of the space as access to the new master and adding a second, small bathroom–again in bead board and with a shower instead of a tub.
- Installation of a second floor washer and dryer.
- New windows, almost as large as the French doors in the family room and kitchen.
- Forgoing the usual contemporary walk-in closet, a closet wall was added to the master bedroom across the width of the space, providing plenty of space while minimizing the intrusion into the bedroom.
- All doors, window trim and cove molding were added to match the original look of the house.

Compromises in materials, fixtures, cabinets, tile, appliances and countertops were agreed to, as they could be upgraded in the future. The primary issue was to maintain the period style in the new addition.

The Solutions

The homeowners negotiated an arrangement whereby they would do some of the work themselves. All skilled work remained with the contractor. The homeowners assembled a team of friends, neighborhoods and college students to help. They agreed to take on all demolition work, site preparation, purchasing materials and site maintenance. Since the couple decided to stay in the house during renovation, they saved money and were able to make sure that the site was secure and well-maintained.

They decided early on that they would ask for help only on larger projects: removing the old driveway, removing the brick bump-out, cleaning and stacking the brick, and removing the roof and siding to the garage. It was agreed that the couple would have one month before the contractor began work.

The demolition was the easiest part of the work. Removing large chunks of concrete, cleaning brick and removing all the garbage strewn around the site proved to be the most difficult. The real surprise was cleaning and recycling face brick, which turned out to be far more work than anticipated. Luckily, the brick was not needed until the very end of the renovation.

The homeowners made sure that something was done every night, even if it was simply taking materials to a dumpster. In the end, as the deadline for their work fast approached, they hired more college students for an entire weekend to help with the heavy lifting–getting concrete and other materials into the dumpster. Despite everyone's effort, the reconstruction started almost a week later than anticipated.

Six months later, the stucco and new driveway were completed, but the garage roof remained unfinished–only sealed with rolled tar paper–and will need to wait. In the end, the interior and exterior spaces were a dead ringer for the original house; the smaller rooms of the older portion of the house flowed nicely into the new space with continuity of flooring, wall treatments, window trim and cove molding.

The Resources

The renovation and restoration of older, period homes is a tricky business. There are a number of good guides available at *www.amazon.com* or *www.barnesandnoble.com.* Among them are:

- *Creating a New Old House: Yesterday's Character for Today's House* (Taunton Press, 2003) has five-star ratings from readers and features 18 period homes with pictures and text.
- *Renovating Old Houses: Bringing New Life to Vintage Homes* (Taunton Press, 2003) tells readers how to make old houses convenient and livable by today's standards. Readers gave the book five stars.
- *New Old House with Reclaimed Materials* (Gibbs Smith, 2005) is a perfect guide for those who want to ensure that reclaimed and recycled materials are used in renovation.

Final Remodeling Punch List

The Challenge

The work is almost finished, with the emphasis on the word *almost*. As every experienced remodeler knows, particularly when the job was long and complicated, there are a dozen small things that need attention, some after the fact.

No matter how hard you look, no matter how careful the workers were, no matter how high-quality their work, there are always little things that need to be finished, repaired or replaced. Your challenge is to make sure that you are satisfied with the work and to secure a firm commitment from the contractor that all the small items on your punch list will be done.

The Facts

You are most likely to get these items taken care of if you bring them up before the final payment and while the workers (or at least some of them) are still on the work site. This is why it is so important not to make the final payment until you have checked everything and gone over anything that needs attention.

Besides the completed work, the work site itself needs to be thoroughly inspected (assuming that you personally are not responsible for general house cleaning).

In The Solutions section on the next page, you will find a master checklist for a variety of projects and work sites. An electronic version of this form can be found at *www.encouragementpress.com*; and are free of charge. You do not need to register, but you are asked to provide your e-mail address on a voluntary basis.

The Solutions

HOMEOWNERS REMODELING PUNCH LIST			
	Date inspected	Date fixed	Call back
Bathroom			
Tub/shower surround			
Water pressure			
Floor tile/pattern			
Wall tile/pattern			
Grout for all tile			
Correct fixtures/match			
Correct bowls/toilet			
Cabinet/countertop			
Lighting/placement/fixture			
Dinners			
GFI/number/spacing			
In-floor heating			
Grab bars			
Shower door fit			
Storage cabinet/fit/plumb			
Window/skylight			
Caulking			
Exhaust fan/placement/size			
Entry door/fit/style			
Wall trim spec/caulked/finished			
Wall finishes—paper/paint			
Final cleaning			
Kitchen			
Cabinets/quality/fit			
Counters/quality/height			
Trim/cabinet spacers			
Windows/skylights			
Counter tops/quality/fit			
Backsplash/quality/fit			
Flooring/quality/fit			
Spacing/work areas			
GFI/number			
General lighting			
Task lighting			
Dimmers			
Appliances/quality/functioning			
Windows/skylights			
Caulking			
Window/door trim/paint/stain			

Wall trim/paint/stain			
Built-ins			
Paint/wallpaper			
Final cleaning			
Family Room			
Fireplace/code/draw			
Log lighter/flue closer/enclosure			
General lighting			
Task lighting			
Wall sconces/splash/picture			
Built-ins/finish/function			
Windows/skylights			
Trim/caulking			
Wood flooring/even stain/finish			
Carpeting/padding			
Room/window trim/paint/stain			
Walls paint/paper			
Doors/stained/painted/placed			
Trim/painted/stained/caulked			
Door and window hardware			
Window treatments			
Final cleaning			
Bedroom, Home Office, Dining Room			
General light			
Task lighting			
Sconces			
Dimmers			
Built-ins/paint/stain			
Wood floors/stain/finish			
Carpeting/quality/color			
Windows/skylights			
Outlets/placement			
Wall/door trim/paint/stain			
Wall treatment/paint/stain			
DSL/cable/phone lines			
Basement			
Mold and mildew removal			
Waterproofing			
Insulation			
Adequate ceiling support			
General lighting			
Task/spot light			
GFI/quantity			
Ventilation/heating			

Stairs/second egress			
Head clearance			
Wall treatment/paint/stain			
Flooring/tile/grout			
Bathroom (see above)			
Bedroom (see above)			
Home office (see above)			
Cable installation			
DSL			
Sump pump			
Dehumidifier			
Cabinets/built-ins/quality/finish			
Ceiling/treatment/insulation			
Window/open/size/privacy			
Separation from utilities			
Storage space			
Attic			
Adequate support			
Insulation			
Access/ease/clearance			
Railing around stairs			
Windows/skylights			
Caulking/trim			
Built-ins			
Head clearance			
Heating/air conditioning/adequate			
General lighting			
Task lighting			
Cable/DSL/phone line(s)			
Additions/external			
Foundation cured/rebar/cracks			
Waterproofing/insulation			
Tied to house/electrical/HVAC			
Soil level/drainage			
Site recovery			
Plant/shrub/tree damage			
Siding/stucco/brick			
Roofing/match/tied-in			

The Resources

To gain access to these and other forms throughout this book, visit *www.encouragementpress.com* to learn more about other Encouragement Press books and products. All forms are free to our readers.

The Celebration

The Challenge

Now that the work is done, the mess cleaned up, the paint fresh and the new rooms gleaming, it is time for a little celebration. You put a lot of work and commitment into this renovation, so you will want to show it off to the world–and make your best friends jealous to boot.

The Facts

It is difficult to stage a party for a large- to medium-sized group. If you follow the practice of *This Old House*, even the contractor and workers are invited! That is usually quite a crowd. Your house-warming need not be so elaborate, but even a basic open house will require a good deal of effort and planning.

Formal dinner parties are difficult to stage and usually require a sit-down dinner. Rather than pulling out all the china and crystal, why not consider an informal brunch on a Sunday afternoon. The menu offered here can be staged buffet-style so that guests can circulate around the house or even outside if the weather permits.

The Solution

Send formal invitations rather than call on the phone. After all, you are in effect having a second house-warming. It is now the custom for friends to ask what they can bring to social gatherings. While generous and thoughtful, this is one time that you should insist that guests come empty-handed. There will be plenty for everyone and this brunch is relatively easy to assemble.

The Sunday Brunch

Bloody Mary Bar

Let guests prepare a drink to their own taste: salty, spicy, with or without alcohol. Have a large chilled pitcher with the best-quality tomato juice (or other seasoned tomato blends) and chilled glasses. Prepare thinly sliced lemon wedges, sliced celery as a stir, and firm, young asparagus spears for additional flavor. Have a large supply of ice with tongs and the best vodka you can afford. For garnish, include course salt, cracked pepper, pepper sauce and Worcestershire sauces. Make sure that a good supply of celery salt is available to top off the Bloody Mary. Start with vodka and ice in tall glasses and then pour the juice. Add goodies to taste.

Mimosas

This is an easy, elegant and refreshing brunch favorite. Fresh-squeezed orange juice is a must along with a nice, very cold champagne or sparkling wine. Ask a guest to be in charge of the champagne, opening bottles only as necessary to keep it fresh and bubbly. Pour the juice first, and then add the wine to taste. This is great excuse to put out the fine crystal for a very elegant presentation!

Bagels, cream cheese, tomatoes and thin sliced onions

Try to avoid the grocery store version bagels; they tend to be soft and unappetizing. If you cannot find a deli locally, some of the chains have decent bagels. Buy a nice selection, from plain to salt, poppy seed, rye, raisin and garlic. Have them sliced and even toasted (you can put them on a cookie sheet in the oven) or have the toaster as part of the buffet. Serve several kinds of cream cheese (plain, chive and strawberry, for example) and have plenty of thinly sliced fresh, firm tomatoes and sweet onions (Walla Walla sweets or other seasonal specialties). Let your guests build their own bagels.

Smoked salmon with capers

Nothing goes better with bagels and cream cheese than smoked salmon (or lox) garnished with capers. The best salmon or lox is hand-sliced and very thin. Spread it out on the platter so it is easy for guests to add to their bagels. Make the slices manageable, to fit the bagel.

Fresh fruit

Whether presented in a half-watermelon boat or your best serving piece, make sure that the fruit is as fresh as fresh can be. Melon balls of all kinds, strawberries, blueberries, raspberries, varieties of grapes off the stems, orange or tangerine slices topped with sliced bananas make a great presentation. Avoid apple and pear slices, as they turn brown quickly without lemon juice.

Sausage and egg casserole

The beauty of this wonderful, homey dish is that is prepared the night before. You will need:

1 pound sausage	1 cup sharp grated cheddar cheese
1½ cups milk	6 slices bread, cubed
1 teaspoon dry mustard	6 eggs, beaten

1. Cube the bread and place in the bottom of a greased casserole dish.
2. Fry and drain the sausage; chop into fine pieces.
3. Beat the eggs; add cheese, milk and dry mustard.
4. Sprinkle the sausage over the bread, and then add the egg mixture.
5. Cover and chill overnight.
6. Put the dish in a cold oven and set the temperature at 350°.
7. Bake for 40 minutes.

Hash brown potato casserole

This dish takes only about 20 minutes to prepare and 45 minutes to cook.
You will need:

> 1 package (2 pounds) frozen hash brown potatoes
> 1 stick of melted butter or margarine   2 cups of sour cream
> ½ cup of finely chopped union   1 teaspoon of salt
> 1 can (10¾ ounces) of cream of chicken soup   Seasoned breadcrumbs
> 8 oz. of grated cheddar cheese
> ½ teaspoon of freshly ground pepper

1. Heat the oven to 350°.
2. Combine potatoes, the melted butter, sour cream, onion soup, cheese, salt and pepper; mix well.
3. Pour the mixture into a buttered 2-quart casserole.
4. Sprinkle breadcrumbs evenly over the top.
5. Bake until hot and bubbly, about 45 minutes.

French toast casserole

This, too, can be prepared ahead of time; put it in the oven about an hour before serving.

You will need these simple ingredients:

> 1 long loaf of French bread   8 large eggs
> 3 cups of milk   4 teaspoons of sugar
> ¾ teaspoon of salt   1 tablespoon of vanilla extract
> Cinnamon
> 2 tablespoons butter or margarine, cut into small pieces
> Maple syrup, honey or powered sugar for topping

1. Butter a 13 x 9 inch baking dish.
2. Cut the bread into 1-inch-thick slices and arrange the bread in a single layer over the bottom of the dish.
3. Beat eggs, milk, sugar, sale and vanilla until mixed and pour over the bread.
4. Cover the banking dish and refrigerate.
5. When ready to serve, dot the top with butter pieces and sprinkle with cinnamon.
6. Bake in a preheated oven at 350° for 45 minutes, or until the bread is puffy and

lightly browned.

(Note: if you are using a glass or ceramic dish directly from the refrigerator, do not preheat the oven. Place the dish in the cold oven and allow an extra 10 or 20 minutes baking time).

Coffee cake

A simple puff pastry Danish will delight the crowd. All you need is:

1 package puff pastry	4 ounces of cream cheese, softened
1 egg	2 tablespoons sugar
A few drops of vanilla extract	½ cup of your favorite preserves

1. Flatten both sheets of puff pastry slightly with a rolling pin.
2. Place each sheet on an ungreased baking sheet.
3. Whip cream cheese, egg, sugar and vanilla until smooth.
4. Divide the mixture evenly between the dough, spreading lightly to within ½ inch of the edges.
5. Top with the preserves.
6. Bake at 400° for 20 to 25 minutes until golden brown.

Coffee and tea

Splurge on the coffee, getting it freshly ground from a gourmet shop. Ditto for the tea. Experiment with a variety of exotic tea bags. Have a pot of boiling hot water at the ready with fresh cream and lump sugar for guests to help themselves.

The Resources

This menu may or may not serve your needs. All the major TV stations feature expert and celebrity chiefs on their programs, and the recipes are always found on their respective Websites. There are several excellent cookbooks available with delightful, easy-to-make goodies to celebrate your new house. Consider two favorites: *Emeril's Potluck: Comfort Food with a Kicked-Up Attitude* by Emeril Lagasse (William Morrow, 2004) and *The Gourmet Cookbook*, edited by Ruth Reichl (Houghton Mifflin, 2004). But this is, of course, just the start. Visit www. *amazon.com* and be ready to be overwhelmed.

ENJOY YOUR NEW, RENOVATED HOME!

Index

Smart, Friendly and Informative

The *50 plus one* series are thorough and detailed guides covering a wide range of topics—both personal and business related, supplying you, the reader, the information and resources you need and want in an easy-to-read format.

50 plus one Greatest Cities In the World You Should Visit
by Paul J. Christopher

Part travel book, part wish book. *50 plus one Greatest Cities in the World You Should Visit* is an intimate, easy and satisfying visit to the world's most wonderful cities. Making plans to travel? Just curious about what makes the world tick? Want to learn more about the great cultural, artistic, culinary and business centers of the world? This is the perfect book for you.

50 plus one Greatest Sports Heroes of All Times (North American Edition)
by Paul J. Christopher

Hold It! You really think we can come up with the greatest sports heroes of all time? Well, we can and we have! Our heroes cut across all sports and are not limited to the most popular spectator sports. On occasion our heroes go back several generations, not just the names in the papers or the sports talk shows.

50 plus one Tips to Building a Retirement Nest Egg
by Linda M. Magoon and Poonum Vasishth

50 plus one Tips to Building a Retirement Nest Egg shows you how in concise, understandable and practical language how to prepare for your financial future. You do not need a financial planner or stockbroker to get started. All you need is the will to turn around your financial well-being and the help tips this book offers.

50 plus one Ways to Improve Your Study Habits.
by Stephen Edwards

Learn the importance of regular study time, create a study environment that is free of distractions and learn the importance of personal organization. Everyone who is trying to improve their academic standing needs help and this easy-to-use book with handy, practical tips is just the ticket.

50 plus one Tips When Hiring & Firing Employees
Edited by Linda M. Magoon & Donna de St. Aubin

Hiring a new employee is one of the most important and time-consuming tasks a manager or entrepreneur can undertake. Firing an employee is an emotionally draining and difficult action, no matter the length of service or level of responsibility. *Hiring & Firing* shows you how to hire the right people for the job and fire those that do not work out, and avoid litigation.

50 plus one Questions When Buying a Car
by Stephen Edwards

50 plus one Questions When Buying a Car is the perfect self-help guide for every potential car buyer, whether you are buying new or pre-owned vehicles. How do you tell if a used car was in an accident? What features on a new car provide good values? What is the best way to finance a car? This book could save you hundreds or thousands of dollars over the many cars you will buy in your lifetime.

50 plus one Tips to Preventing Identity Theft
by Elizabeth Drake

50 plus one Tips to Preventing Identity Theft is your first step to protecting your family, your money and your identity. This book is particularly important if you travel internationally or buy on the Internet. The more complicated your financial life, the more vulnerable you may be and the more important this book is to keeping your finances secure.

50 plus one Great Books You Should Have Read (and probably didn't)
by George Walsh

50 plus one Great Books You Should Have Read (and probably didn't) is a masterpiece of information for individuals who want to expand their horizons or simply impress friends. Walsh and his advisory panel selected literary works, which have had the greatest impact on writing, government, international politics, religion, and the arts and sciences. International in scope, the books chosen for this list have survived centuries and are considered essential for a liberal education.

50 plus one Questions to Ask Your Doctor
by Elizabeth Drake

You are in a hurry to get to the doctor's office. The doctor too, is pressed for time; the waiting room is full and time is of the essence. Under the pressure, you forget to ask the questions or seek further advice that you have been meaning to ask. *50 plus one Questions to Ask Your Doctor* is a simple, clear, practical and up-to-date; take it to the doctor's office with you as a reminder of what you need to discuss.

Titles from Encouragement Press

Available from bookstores everywhere or directly from Encouragement Press. Bulk discounts are available, for information please call 1.253.303.0033

50 plus one Series			
Title	Price	Qty.	Subtotal
Greatest Cities in the World You Should Visit	$14.95 U.S./$19.95 Can.		
Tips When Remodeling Your Home	$14.95 U.S./$19.95 Can.		
Greatest Sports Heroes of All Times (North American Edition)	$14.95 U.S./$19.95 Can.		
Tips to Building A Retirement Nest Egg	$14.95 U.S./$19.95 Can.		
Ways To Improve Your Study Habits	$14.95 U.S./$19.95 Can.		
Tips When Hiring & Firing Employees	$14.95 U.S./$19.95 Can.		
Questions When Buying a Car	$14.95 U.S./$19.95 Can.		
Tips to Preventing Identity Theft	$14.95 U.S./$19.95 Can.		
Great Books You Should Have Read (and probably didn't)	$14.95 U.S./$19.95 Can.		
Questions to Ask Your Doctor	$14.95 U.S./$19.95 Can.		

Subtotal	
IL residents add 8.75% sales tax	
Shipping & Handling*	
Total	

* Shipping & Handling

U.S. Orders:	Canadian Orders:
$3.35 for first book	$7.00 for first book
$2.00 for ea. add'l book	$5.00 for ea. add'l book

4 Ways to Order

Phone: 1.773.262.6565

Web: *www.encouragementpress.com*

Fax: 1.773.262.9765

Mail: Encouragement Press LLC
1261 W. Glenlake
Chicago, IL 60660

Please make checks payable to:
Encouragement Press, LLC
(Orders must be prepaid. We regret that we are unable to ship orders without payment or purchase order)

Payment Method (check one)
❏ **Check enclosed** ❏ **Visa** ❏ **MasterCard**

_____
card number

_____
signature

_____
Name as it appears on card

expiration date _____

P.O. #_____

Encouragement Press, LLC
1261 W. Glenlake • Chicago, IL 60660 • *sales@encouragementpress.com*